MOTORCYCLE
SURVIVOR

MOTORCYCLE SURVIVOR

Tips and Tales in the Unrestored Realm

KRIS PALMER

PARKER
HOUSE

Parker House Publishing Inc.,
1826 Tower Drive, Stillwater,
Minnesota 55082, USA
www.parkerhousepublishing.com

ISBN-13: 978-0-9817270-9-7

Book and cover design: Diana Boger
Cover design concept: Amy Van Ert-Anderson
Editor: Kristal Leebrick

Manufactured in China through World Print

10 9 8 7 6 5 4 3 2 1

For the gang from Spring Mill Farms,
where old wrenches and youthful optimism
frequently collided…and sometimes
made something run.

Contents

LAP 1: SURVIVOR TIPS

LAP 2: SURVIVOR TALES

WIDE OPEN THROTTLE

YANKEE IRON

FOR A GOOD HOME, CALL...

Beach Battle Echoes…

When KR Ruled Daytona

MOTORSPORTS LEGENDS DIDN'T court public attention, they seized it—thrashing overvamped wheelbound bombs a few revs, a few molecules of tenacious tire tread, from fiery, bone-smashing oblivion. What separates any bike from all others are the wars it has waged, the miles it has run. Survivors show their scars. Even when the air is still, you can hear their engines howl. The sounds of some, raced by giants, never go silent.

Merely on the strength of the photograph at left of the ex-Floyd Emde KR Harley, I would buy this book. What memories. Memories that are more than visual. I can almost hear the amazing beast sounding off as I did a long time ago. You could judge how aggressively a K was being raced just from the waves of sound it was making. All of them were bred for sound. Bred for Daytona Beach.

Not the Daytona of this century but the Daytona of the fifties, when the season's 200-mile brawl was fought over a sand and coral oval battleground four miles long right along the Atlantic. Sand swirled and blasted faces. Startled shore birds buzzed riders. And gassing a dreadnaught K up to and in excess of maybe 135 miles per hour without benefit of vision was another part of the beachfront mystique.

And then there was Jungle Road, Daytona's shrub-strewn back straightaway. Barely two lanes wide, it sprouted bushes as big as houses. Jousting K models took its undulating measure while grappling three and four abreast in hell-bent wolf packs.

Pavement laid on top of asphalt, the road was marked by violent dips and rises assailing riders for two interminable miles. The whole nerved-up experience on Jungle Road boiled down to a speed wobble. A rider needed colossal talent to meet a K's demands barreling wide-open into such godforsaken terrain.

The heavy gauge Ks with their museum piece side valves were quite famous in their own right. One especially noble engine won Daytona four times, as well as four Laconias, and always set top qualifying time. And in 1964, three long years after the 200 miles had moved inside Daytona International Speedway, the same engine raised a familiar battle cry and set fast time all over again.

A fiercely competitive streak ran through all K riders, but especial those on Harley's factory racing team. And also among the many factory tuners building up the K. All of them boasted about making the most K horsepower. In 1968, which became the next-to-last season of model K superiority, the factory tuner who was on top was named Roy Bokelman.

Part of the reason Bokelman was on top was because his jockey was Freddy Nix, at 118 pounds the most flyweight flyer in the Harley factory arsenal. The very first time that Bokelman and Nix combined, at Springfield, for the National of 1965, Nix broke the mile track speed record.

Their first win at a National came in 1966, when Nix took the important step of stopping the Gold Star BSA of Sammy Tanner from trashing Harley-Davidson prestige on the Sacramento mile.

The big, unbelievable, season of Bokelman and Nix was 1968.

Life at the Motor Company was in ruin following 1967, which was Harley's most humiliating season in 13 years. Milwaukee had won only eight of 17 national championship races and lost the Grand National championship to Triumph.

Failure followed everybody up. The K engine Bokelman put together was in response to Harley losing the No. 1 plate. Arguably the most over-powered K ever, all its speed goodies got laid out on a precision bore machine right in Bokelman's Milwaukee home and laboratory. It was an engine a runner builds but once in his life. And it was a pounder. When it blew off Gary Nixon's No. 1 Triumph by 15 mph across the Daytona bankings, its sound must have made Nixon wonder whether he had just been passed by an airplane. Other motorcycles merely blasted, but Freddy Nix had this one roaring in some previously unknown stratosphere. You could hear it coming over the top of even the other K's.

Freddy had no fear of it. Winning a pair of dirt track Nationals and all four of the tournament's mile meets made Nix racing's new hero. His exploits at Portland, Santa Rosa, Sedalia, and Sacramento were breathtaking runaways. Next he used the explosive force to surmount a leading Triumph and win high off Oklahoma City's dry slick last corner.

Nix's reign ended in Los Angeles at Ascot Park's 1968 finale. This was the national race that haunted him. He selected the wrong rear tire, one that chunked its tread. The Triumph tribe raced up to smother him and cost Nix and Harley the Grand National title by a fistful of points.

Roy Bokelman's big K had been heard, however. It had been heard too damn well. In 1969 a claque of Brits had come to power within the sanctioning body, and, simmering from years of resentment and defeat, they vowed to avenge themselves on the flathead Ks by granting their own overhead Triumphs and BSAs with duplicate 750cc displacement.

Predictably the fantastic K held off the Queen of England's avengers. First Bokelman's K beat the redcoats on the long mile of Nazareth. Then it won in a lashing rainstorm at Loudon. But then came the fall.

For the two seasons, 1970 and 1971, before Harley got its new alloy XR up and dominant, the English had their way, with Triumphs and BSAs winning so many Nationals they drowned out the memory of the K.

Even the most ominous K of them all, the Bokelman K, slowly lost its pedigree, and its ability to win national races. It ended up in regional skirmishes, but finally couldn't win there either. The end came when its full-race cylinders received their last over-bore. This was one of the many drawbacks of the antique K: the ports are part of the cylinders. Upon reaching maximum bore, there really was nothing to do but discard them.

So the engine got sold as damaged goods to a Harley dealership in Knoxville, Tennessee, who bartered it to a friend who owned an immaculate K model licensed for street use. On the boulevards is where the great Bokelman K presumably died.

As the sovereign of the mile tracks, Freddy played the role of real cool dude to the point of wearing a set of shades while racing. He wasn't a real cool dude. He was just a farmer's son from unworldly Lawton. He was a good guy and deserving of a far better fate than getting into a stupid head-on wreck on a narrow winding road in the central California mountains. Freddy Nix died in the summer of 1969 at the wheel of a cheesy-sounding dune buggy—Freddy, the maker of the hottest motorcycle sounds of the 1960s!

R.I.P., Bokelman K. R.I.P., Freddy.

Acknowledgements

THE FOLLOWING PEOPLE PROVIDED their time, expertise, patience, hospitality, references, and no small number of beautiful motorcycles, scooters, minibikes, and related getabouts to help transform the following ideas and stories into a finished book. Thanks for your generosity and patience: Tom Jones, Lucy Bacon, Tim Parker, Rick Wyatt, Jerry Lee, Denny and Kari Kannenberg, Kim and John Bones, Pat and Cris Simmons, Steve Hamel, Gene Berghoff, Deke Diegal, Del Hofer, Tim O'Keeffe, John Eiden, Logan Coombs, Joe Scalzo, Norm Mosher, and Bob, Sid, and Scott Chantland.

Jerry Lee has been snapping professional photographs for 27 years. *Sports Illustrated, Sporting News, NCAA* and major college publications and newspapers around the country have featured his images. Jerry's sharp, detailed photography has also appeared in Motorbook's *How to Repair Your Car, How to Repair Your SUV,* and Parker House's *Survivor: The Unrestored Collector Car.*

The author's 1983 CB1100F
wears performance stickers
on the quarter-fairing
and swingarm. They will
stay, as will original paint.
Aftermarket goodies fitted
long ago will stay too, or be
swapped with NOS parts.

Introduction

MOTORCYCLE DEALERSHIPS are great places to while away an hour or an afternoon hopping saddles, staring, and dreaming. I just bought a 1983 Honda CB1100F, a bike I first saw on the showroom floor at a dealership in Newark, Delaware, the year the model was released in the United States. With its taut, aerodynamic lines and huge engine, it stayed fresh in my mind for more than 25 years. When I recently saw one for sale at Sport Wheels in Jordan, Minnesota, I decided to buy it on the spot.

It isn't perfect. It's a quarter-century old! It has some chips, scratches, and fading. The header pipes have cooked off their paint and developed a fine layer of brown rust. The tires are old and worn (and will be replaced). The original seat has been swapped out, as have the handgrips. It has stickers on it. It doesn't gleam. "Looks like new" is not a phrase that applies any longer.

Yet the bike is not the least bit less appealing to me than the day I saw the model fresh, unridden, perfect, with zeroes across the odometer. It has aged like we all have and covered thousands of miles. I did not buy it to store or display. I bought it to ride, and those signs of age make it that much easier.

Seized anew with this burning desire to own the bike that had captivated me as a teenager, I could have saved my pennies and combed the Internet, looking for one that had been immaculately restored. But I'd rather have this one. Bugs will hit it, and gravel and rain. A kid or a car might bump it and tip it over.

Perfection is so fragile. Patina is forever.

Somehow, the bike that wears its years is more intriguing, more genuine, than the one returned to a condition it knew only in a time long passed. Restored bikes are beautiful to look at and appreciate, and often to ride, too, with everything revamped, repadded, recalibrated. Still, many of us are more seduced by the bike sitting dusty in a shed than the same model flawless on a museum floor.

This book is the second on the survivor phenomenon from Parker House. *Survivor: The Unrestored Collector Car* came out in December 2008. We've done our best to flesh out the ideas and provide exciting examples and stories embodying the nature and spirit of unrestored motorcycles.

Survivor bikes are unique animals, fundamentally different from other categories of motorcycles, like two strokes and four strokes, race bikes or choppers. Facts in this context are most relevant with any particular bike, rather than unrestored motorcycles as a class. For this reason, *Motorcycle Survivor* is a book of ideas and tales, rather than a catalog of specifications or values. Naming the best unrestored bike, or the most desirable or valuable, is like picking the greatest racer or the coolest dude or woman ever to swing a leg over an iron horse. Those arguments are better at a cafe sitting among the bikes and some good friends in the sun, knocking back a thick black coffee.

Motorcycle survivors are artifacts preserving their build methodology and use history. They hold stories and secrets, known, forgotten, and yet to be discovered. Each survivor stands on its own, and it is precisely that characteristic that makes them so appealing.

You could hunt the classifieds and collector haunts and find two '57 Harley Sportsters—or two 1974 Ossa 250 Moto-cross Phantoms, take them to the same restoration shop, and ask that they be restored identically, bolt for bolt, wire for wire. With every part blasted, polished, painted, or replaced in the same way, by the same people with the same products, you could achieve that goal. But you cannot find two that are identical before they are restored.

The survivor bikes will vary in hundreds of ways, from the obvious—a scratch or chip here, a ding there, a performance sticker, mileage—to the subtle—one has faded just a bit more on the tank or the gauge faces; another has dry rot on the footpeg covers or leather seat. The wear might have an interesting source. Maybe the left-side handgrip has a few road-rash marks on it where the original owner tipped it over trying to stand on the seat to hang a new net on a basket-ball rim for a neighbor kid named Larry Bird or Julius Erving. Or maybe the fender has a few drill holes in it because the first owner, in a fit of teen romanticism, put his girlfriend's initials there with push-in chrome letters decades before. The marks each unrestored motorcycle has that are different from those of all other bikes, and that document its owners' adventures, form the essence of the survivor concept.

In this book, we explore what a survivor is, ideas and influences that affect the decision of whether to keep a bike unrestored, and many examples of survivor bikes, from the ultra rare and valuable to more accessible machines that are just as appealing in their patina-ed state. Ace snapper Jerry Lee and I have done our best to capture the essence of these bikes with his crisp and detailed photographs.

Because the wear and aging that characterizes unrestored bikes is inextricable from the people who have bought, ridden, and collected them—and these riders are to thank for keeping them that way—the book also tells the stories of numerous owners and their survivor machines. Their tales and their bikes evoke our collective experiences admiring and enjoying the motorized bicycle, from spindly cente-narian to modern burly ballistic.

Lap I, Survivor Tips, looks at originality, preservation, and resto-ration ideas and issues.

Lap II, Survivor Tales, tells the stories of many unrestored bikes and the owners who cherish them.

We hope something here will strike a note that resonates like the pipes on a favorite bike and maybe prompts a few people to look at dust and dings and crow-footed paint in a new light. Enjoy it, and thanks for making *Motorcycle Survivor* a part of your enthusiast library.

—Kris Palmer 2009

Author's note: Including the publisher's Laverda 750 SFC was not his idea; it was mine. I had seen it years before, owner unknown, and wheedled the story and some cool early photos out of Tim Parker, once I knew it was his.

"Lost time is never found again."
—*Benjamin Franklin*

LAP 1:
SURVIVOR
TIPS

A flood of low-priced Japanese bikes left this Harley-Davidson Aermacchi Leggero unsold. Even in warehouse storage, environmental forces dry rotted the battery hold-down strap.

CHAPTER 1

Patina

Approve or Remove?

"Restored" and "preserved" are like motion and stillness. You can have either, but you cannot have both. Only when the unrestored bike is new do the two states look virtually identical. As soon as the factory paint dries and assembly workers turn the last bolt, the forces of entropy attack and start the long, slow—or short, fast—process of removing shine and "newness."

Moisture, sunlight, smoke, fire, mold, airborne contaminants, oxidation, rodents, insects, and temperature and humidity swings and extremes can wreak havoc on paint, sheet metal, leather, textiles, tires, gaskets, belts, chains, fluids, bearings, seals, and any other unprotected surface or component.

Paintwork loses its luster and begins to fade. Encounters with snaps, buckles, rivets, basketballs, falling rakes and shovels and brooms, bicycles, keys, watches, bracelets, rings, dropped wrenches, screwdrivers, and bolts leave their dings, scratches, and dents. Stones and gravel chip the finish; chemicals, soft drinks, and bird-droppings leave spots. Prolonged polishing wears off the paint, and moisture—with its accomplices, mud and salt—savages exposed metal into open rusty sores. Every day that passes sustains existing destructive forces and creates opportunity for new ones.

Deterioration occurs even if the motorcycle isn't used. There are a few bikes in this book that were never put on the road. Still, they show age's marks—in some cases more than the nicest low-mileage bikes, washed, polished, and protected.

The question, then, is what to do about it. How much wear and damage in a valued possession are we willing to tolerate? For the devoted unrestored vehicle fan, it may be quite a lot, but imperfection

Once begun, a thorough restoration effort would include binning the rubber on this kick starter. It's ironic that the age marks prompting the swap would resemble the lines in the hands doing the scrapping.

isn't a state all of us accept naturally and to the same degree. How many of us would wear a threadbare coat on a date? Or a shirt with stains? Shoes with holes? We don't wear motorcycles, but we appear with them. They are reflections of ourselves. That fact can weigh on our decisions more than we realize.

Every day around the globe restorers are tearing into bikes that some owners would leave—and cherish—just as they are. And the opposite is equally true. There are chipped, flaking, faded bikes with patina and dry rot galore that perfection-minded owners would love to get hold of, to blast, straighten, paint up, and polish like the very day those bikes were assembled and pushed onto a showroom floor. Odds are, most readers of this book have had at least one bike for which the decision of whether to keep the beauty marks, or put everything back in print-ad condition, was not so easy.

Part of the incentive for restoration arises from longstanding perceptions. The words that capture a survivor bike's charm don't sound as good in other contexts: chipped, faded, frayed, rotted, dented, bent, dusty, torn, split, cracked, dull. Why tolerate something in that shape when you can have clean, polished, gleaming, flawless, pristine, shining, immaculate, vibrant, and like new?

When we've known bikes whose plating, paint, rubber, seat, decals, tanks, and fenders are perfect, it takes a certain concession to chaos and mortality to leave them alone as marks and wear pile up.

When we wheeled out this humble Batavus Super Sport to photograph, a few people asked to buy it and more stopped to admire it. The lines rather overstate performance, but it's a beautiful little machine. (The owner has the chain guard, too, which is not shown.)

Who Cares If It's Unrestored?

If shows, auctions, and buzz on the street are any indication—and they are—the answer is that a lot of people do, both those who own motorcycles and those who simply admire interesting objects from another era. Six or seven years ago, I rolled my bike out onto the sidewalk, parked it, and walked back to close the garage door. A silver-haired woman, about 70, was returning to her car from the nearby shops. Suddenly she stopped and stared thoughtfully at the bike, which was still dusty from a winter in storage.

"What kind is it?" she asked.

"It's a 1975 Honda CB750," I said.

"I know nothing of motorcycles," she responded, "but it sure is beautiful."

Of all the comments people have made over the years about that bike, that one stood out because there was no knowledge, no history, no personal connection behind it. This passerby appreciated a 30-year-old motorcycle because of the pleasing convergence of its chrome bars and fenders, mirrors, and wheels, its burnt-orange tank and side covers, its badges with the lettering aged off-white. It didn't matter to her that it was dusty, the seat was split, and there was a crack, repaired, in the rear fender. The bike was what it was, and the impression it made was so strong, she bothered to call out—and that was all she said. Something I owned had affected someone else.

Norm Mosher has taught many new riders the basics with his 1979 Kawasaki 400 LTD, "the flop-a-lot." It's reliable, easy to ride, and doesn't have too much power for novices, though they still manage to tip it over wherever gravity is to be found. Lucy Bacon, right, isn't one of those newbies. She's a Buell rider who owns Diamonds Coffee Shoppe in Minneapolis, a favorite biker watering hole—and a fine spot to begin a journey, a friendship, or a book on unrestored motorcycles.

The pleasure an unrestored bike gives to others is something to consider. On the one hand, our possessions belong to us, and we have absolute power over them. Not only can we strip our bikes down and restore them, we can bury them, crush them, or melt them down and make roofing nails. On the other hand, with even a little protection, a motorcycle of steel, aluminum, plastic, and leather will long outlast a human life. Just as other owners may have passed them on to us, we will leave the motorcycles in our care to future generations. If the paint and lettering, plating and rubber, wires, nuts, washers, and bolts that the workers in a now-defunct factory fitted are still on it, don't they convey more of this artifact's nature, of its source, than modern replacement parts and coatings?

An investment advisor may say that unrestored condition is important only with older, rarer bikes and that leaving those rock chips on your 11-year-old Kawasaki makes little sense if keeping the original paint is your main concern. By the late 1920s, all the great bikes from the teens were about 11 too. The unrestored examples from that era generate a lot of interest today, even the ones made in large numbers at the time. Investments are cast in long and short terms; your bike will outlive both. This is not to say that investment criteria are irrelevant. They're critical if your purpose in collecting motorcycles is to profit from it. But those concerns—and your bike's potential meaning to your descendants or a collector, museum-goer, or historian a century from now—are separate.

Whether to preserve or restore a given bike is a personal decision, yet its consequences extend for the rest of the bike's existence. If you're holding one of only a few unrestored examples of a particular motorcycle, remember that restoring it takes a little bit of history—in its scratches and dings and information—in the materials and methods of its construction, away from posterity.

Even a common bike you ride everyday will have fewer and fewer peers as the decades pass.

Classic bikes that are still in their factory shipping crates, like these CZs from just after World War II, are extremely rare. Sellers and auction houses used to break open the crates, scrap them, and build up the bikes before offering them to the public. Like restoration, that's a move that can't be undone.

A lot of us would enjoy owning a bike with this name on the tank. Too bad the decal's all faded and cracked. Better strip it off and put on a bright, shiny new one, eh? No!!

CHAPTER 2

Good as Old

TELEVISION'S INFLUENCE is waning in the Internet age, but it remains a powerful medium for disseminating ideas, even from unexpected sources. *Antiques Roadshow* began in Britain in the late 1970s and crossed the Atlantic to appear on the U.S. Public Broadcasting System in the 1990s.

Popular hunger for a program about old stuff exceeded its producers' most optimistic projections. The show won an international audience and prompted viewers to poke around their own garages and attics for potential treasures. Frequently, the show's appraisers called out originality as a key value indicator. Unrestored pieces, with the original finish and hardware, enjoyed more praise and a higher estimate. Works by well known artists and crafters that had been stripped and redone were often marked down for that reason.

As the program continued and its audience grew, a broad cross-section of the public took home the notion that restoration hurts value. So strong was this incidental message that the furniture restoration industry felt its impact. The editor of the magazine *Professional Refinishing* wrote the American show's executive producer to describe the influence it was having in his field. The producer's response explained that while their appraisers enjoyed finding rare pieces in good condition, that was not the shape much old furniture was in. Objects with excessive wear or damage typically did benefit from restoration. Even if the public had over-applied the value of unrestored condition, the show gave people pause in reaching for the paint stripper and polyurethane.

Antiques Roadshow popularized the idea of leaving time's indicia alone. Older items are perceived as better made, rarer, more nostalgic and collectible than new products. Original goods are valued more highly than reproductions. If the genuine article is more desirable, why spend time and money removing the very characteristics, like patina, that distinguish it from a modern knockoff? Patina helps prove age, the aspect of a vintage or classic object that inspired our admiration in the first place.

The program's influence in the motorcycle arena was formally recognized when the Motorcycle Hall of Fame Museum credited it with inspiring the museum's "Vintage Triumph Roadshow" during the American Motorcyclist Association's Vintage Motorcycle Days in 2008. Like the TV show, the event included appraisals of unrestored motorcycles, as well as those restored to correct original condition.

Naturally, respect for age and originality predates *Antiques Roadshow*, which merely brought together experts applying views from many fields developed before the show tapped them. Patrick Milan is a Minneapolis-based artisan who repairs stringed instruments. When a damaged violin—for example, one splintered in a car accident—comes into his shop, his first step in addressing it is to study the original wood and varnish and determine the intent of the instrument's maker. "We want to save as much of the original piece as possible," he says. "Even when wood or finish must be replaced, we strive to take away as little as possible and put it back in such a way that it is indistinguishable from the original."

Gun collectors likewise value pieces that have not had their history blasted or stripped away. Bluing, the preservative process giving unpainted gun metal its characteristic look, has been done different ways at different times and places. This finish's condition has a great deal to do with a collector gun's value. Extensive refinishing will harm the value of a rare or historically significant firearm (even if it enhances a common gun that's too rough).

Coin collectors are equally familiar with original appearances and the perils of removing them. Those numismatists who rubbed off tarnish with a pencil eraser learned too late that they had likewise scrubbed value from their collection.

All of these objects—guns, coins, furniture, instruments, and motorcycles—help define the look and feel of the period during which they were made and used in daily life. Remove time's marks, and the object loses its most convincing connection with the past it represents. It becomes a modern interpretation of an old item.

As the popular saying goes, "it's only original once." When you remove the original finish and replace original parts, you destroy some of the connections linking the object's present with its past. Remove all signs of age and wear, and onlookers may wonder how much, if any, of the bike hails from the year of its purported manufacture. Under new paint or chrome, a part stamped out by the original factory in Europe or the United States decades or a century ago may bear precious little clue that it was not made in China with modern tooling last month.

What's in a Name?

Motorcycles are a hobby filled with passion—and jargon. Like other hobbies, this one has its own terms and slang, words other niches don't understand or use in a different way. Even among gearheads and collectors there are some divergent approaches. The survivor concept has fuzzy boundaries, as proven by the many ways sellers, buyers, and owners use it. Fortunately, the related notions of unrestored, preserved and original bikes offer some compass points. Together, they describe important principles for the future of collector motorcycles.

We're using the word to describe an unrestored bike. Part of the concept's blurriness, however, comes from "unrestored" having some definitional play of its own. Does it mean "untouched" or only "not comprehensively restored"? The older a motorcycle gets, the more likely parts and finishes have been replaced or at least repaired. Some of these are maintenance items or "perishables" that must be renewed periodically for functionality and safety. Replace too much of what was

Restorers seek perfection and would therefore resist reproducing the oversight on this BSA Shooting Star. The bike left the factory with a pinstripe separating the red and white paint on one side of the tank but not the other.

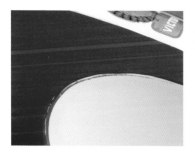

first there, however, and the bike moves further from the "unrestored" condition that most excites patina fans.

"Preserved" gets us a little closer. That which is preserved is predominantly unchanged. "Perfectly preserved" connotes an object frozen in time, one that looks today as it did when last seen or used. Still, what are the parameters that rule a bike in, or out of, this definition? Preserved *in what way*? If the whole bike is there, but it's rusting and the seat is torn up, the gauges are faded and cracked, the engine is stuck, and the handgrips and footpegs are split, is it preserved? In the sense that you can see it, touch it, and identify all of its parts, yes, it's preserved. It has not disappeared, been dismantled, or been destroyed. But if preserved is a state of survival in which collectors should consider leaving the bike for its historic value, this one pushes limits as to the number of faults many enthusiasts would accept over the long haul. A motorcycle in "worn but presentable" condition would appease more owners.

Finally, there's "original," another term that seems a lot more self-explanatory at first glance. *Original owner* is a nice, straightforward term the hobby is in agreement on. We could create ambiguity by suggesting that a dealership owns the bike first, or the manufacturer, but no one understands it that way. The original owner is the one who bought the bike new.

"Original" as applied to the motorcycle takes us back to familiar ambiguous territory. Everyone who reads classified ads has seen listings for bikes characterized as both "all original" and "totally restored." Foremost Insurance (part of Farmers Insurance Group), for example, includes "original restored condition" in its description of "collectible automobile." Before unrestored vehicles started attracting attention at big-time auctions and shows, juxtaposing these statements didn't seem strange. Now, to at least a few people in the hobby, it does. What such a phrase is apparently conveying is that all the major parts—engine, tank, frame, wheels, gauges—are the ones that were on the bike when it was new. Yet if it's been totally restored, many things applied by the factory have disappeared. The original paint has been removed or covered up—totally restored bikes have perfect paint; unrestored ones don't. A lot of restorations also involve scrapping old nuts, bolts,

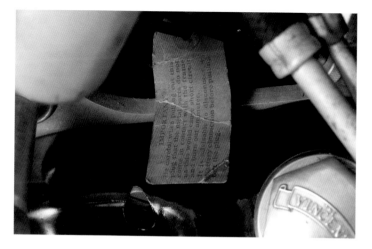

Factory warning labels fitted at delivery but not intended to remain on the bike during use go beyond "unrestored" status. They're unique extras that seldom survive. This original tag is still on Bob Chantland's ultra-original unrestored Black Shadow.

cables, handgrips, badges, wiring, and rubber covers on footpegs, kick starter, shifter . . .

How can a "totally restored" BMW R69 or Moto Morini 3-1/2 or Kawasaki W1 be "all original" when so much of the factory's work has been undone? The answer involves perspective and our collective willingness to exclude some things from the originality inquiry. "Perishables," like brake pads, battery, oil and air filters, tires, and fluids are items that must be replaced to ensure proper functioning and safety. Asking auctioneers of "all-original" bikes to drop the description, or footnote it, when the battery has been replaced goes too far. For those extremely rare bikes that still have such factory-fitted components, owners and sellers can add them to their "all-original" qualifications, pushing them beyond expectations.

Bikes bearing their original maintenance items, along with everything else, would lie at the strictest end of the originality scale. At the other end are motorcycles with their original engines, transmissions, and frames. The laxest use of "numbers-matching bike" means only that the engine in it is the one the factory fitted, and of course not all manufactures matched even these two numbers.

Increased emphasis on bikes that haven't been restored may gradually contract our use of "original" from identity to condition. Under the former sense, a Moto Guzzi mirror is original if it's the one that came on the bike when it was built—or perhaps on another Guzzi of the same model and period. Turn the survivor lens in front of our

Various maintenance and repair jobs involve pulling off the plug wires. How many owners and shops bother to refit them with the original routing and clips? This wonderfully preserved Triumph Speed Twin shows exactly how the factory did it.

A broken headlight is a tough call, but not if you ride the bike. If you can't get an identical NOS light, save the nonfunctional one for display and pop in a bright, safe one for when you hit the roads.

eyes to a higher magnification, and we wonder whether that same mirror, even the one fitted to that specific bike when new, is rightly called "original" when it has been replated. Original in that case means only identity, not condition, because the plating on it today is not what came on it when new.

At a GM car show at the Minnesota state fairgrounds one spring, there was a 1970 'Vette in an uncommon color. The owner said the shade was originally slated for a prior model year, but Chevrolet discovered a color-match problem with touch-up paint prior to production and pulled it. He then said a prior-year Corvette had recently turned up that actually was painted that shade; its paint code identified it as a "pilot" color.

How exciting! And this car is in good, original condition? "Oh no," he responded. "It's getting a total restoration." They're repainting it? "Yes," he said, "in the original color."

Under traditional restoration ideology, this is a logical move: Take that rare vehicle and make it perfect. To the diehard survivor fan, a one-of-a-kind specimen—or at least its one-of-a-kind attribute—is effectively being destroyed. The vehicle's owner is focused on *the fact of the thing* (the car was painted in this shade) over *the thing itself* (the paint). Once that unique paint, sprayed on that vehicle alone some 40 years ago, gets stripped off, the only known paint job of its kind has been undone. The replacement is new paint. It may look like the original once looked; it may be identified by the same paint code. But it's twenty-first century paint, mixed and sprayed by today's equipment and employees beside other shades for vehicles that did not exist when that 'Vette was built. The pilot-color car had probably faded, and that was the rub. The original paint was no longer its original shade. Such are the ambiguities and challenges of preservation decisions.

Even when used for identity, the issue of "original" parts is provocative. To be the Guzzi's original mirror, must it be the very one fitted by a factory worker on that bike during initial assembly? Or is a different one from the same source manufactured the same year still original? If the part was not numbered to coordinate with a particular vehicle, establishing whether it's the exact one originally fitted, or an identical contemporary, may be both impossible—and pointless. It would seem significant only if the one originally installed had some other attribute of uniqueness, for example, custom, one-of-a-kind styling or some mark like a rider's or customizer's initials. Otherwise, if even the top experts in the field can't tell whether it was initially fitted to a specific bike or taken from one a few VIN numbers earlier or later, how important is the difference?

Given the passion in this area, someone will pay more for the all as-fitted bike than the one with a mirror and a headlight from an identical contemporary, but how would you know, without some unique mark, if what you paid for is what you got? "Knowing" it's the original piece may help us sleep better, even if the proof comes down to belief.

Another interesting wrinkle that arises when exploring originality is that people's memories are fallible as to what has and has not been redone. When you talk to an owner about a very original bike, and he or she rattles off what has been replaced, quite frequently one or two more changes pop up if you go and have a look at the motorcycle. You peer here and there and shoot some photos; the owner gazes and appraises with you, and often pipes up with something like, "Oh, and I replaced the taillight lens—it was cracked . . .," or "I added the horn button," or "One wheel had seized spokes and was out of true, so I found another just like it. . . ." These don't come off as admissions of some prior duplicity; they're just things the owner forgot about. Maybe it's human nature to overestimate the qualities we most admire.

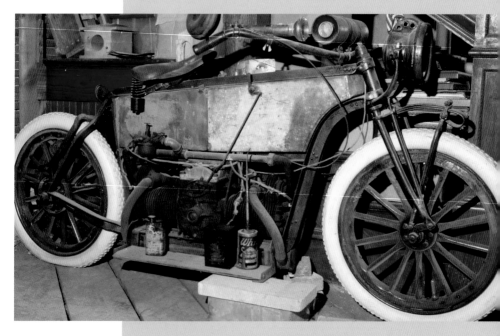

This wooden-wheeled one-off was built by a blacksmith with an angle-iron frame, an early automotive engine, and whatever else he had at hand to make it go. It never looked like a new vehicle. If you restored it, what condition would you "restore" it to?

CHAPTER 3

Value and Worth

GENERALLY, FINE PRESERVED EXAMPLES of collectible objects are worth at least as much as, and often more than, restored examples, but there are caveats. One reflects the ambiguous nature of the term "preserved." Depending on the bike's history, there may have been changes made that not only do not harm the bike's value, they enhance it. Race bikes, customs, vehicles modified by famous people or for a well-known purpose, may be better left in their modified state. To collectors and enthusiasts, these bikes can be original, preserved, and modified all at once. The important "original" state is the one to which it was taken for its most significant use.

Pushed to their limit every time out, race bikes get rebuilt and repaired constantly. Parts get bent, they break, and they get patched, welded, painted, swapped out, and swapped back with highest performance reigning over all other concerns. When an unrestored race bike comes up for sale, particularly one with a long history, it will not bear all of the components initially fitted from the manufacturer. It may present very few of them. The typical goals in restoration—flat surfaces, perfect paint, shiny plating, and unbent, unbroken parts—lie particularly distant from the bike as acquired. Scrapping what is imperfect here is like sanitizing a crime scene or rewriting history, wiping away much of the madness and chaos that characterized the bike's prior, glorious life.

Customized bikes, like bobbers and choppers, that characterize an era or feature the work of a well-known builder, raise comparable concerns. These bikes are becoming very popular. In determining whether the bike is "original" enough, or in sufficiently good condition, it's best to base the decision on the bike's special circumstances. Blasting

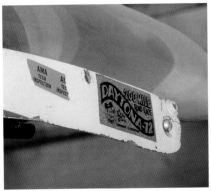

Stripping and painting this fairing would destroy two pieces of this Kawasaki racer's history: stickers indicating that the bike passed AMA tech inspection and that it competed in the Daytona 200 of 1972. While a graphic artist could replicate them, counterfeits wouldn't have the cool-factor of the real items.

off a storied customizer's paint or pin striping because it's faded or polished thin in spots could be an expensive decision. Those are the details that make the bike exciting.

Movie bikes may disappoint fans of gleam and polish. Shiny brilliance—glare—is mostly undesirable on a movie screen. The director and editor want to guide your eye to the portion of the screen they feel is important. If "light artifacts" are radiating off the bike's gas tank or handlebars, that's what the audience will look at—like an abandoned soldier signaling a passing plane with a piece of glass. Movie vehicles are often painted with a dull finish, or spritzed with a liquid to diffuse and mute the light. This bland paint, often hand-brushed—plus gaffer's tape and other quirks applied to aid filming, may encourage the typical buyer to strip it down and make it look good, like it did onscreen. Survivor fans would prefer it in "original" movie condition—the way it was when it produced the footage moviegoers watched and appreciated.

When you get a special bike of this sort, proceed slowly and carefully. Compare what you like and dislike about the way it looks with the parts or features that make it unique. If the bike's aesthetic challenges relate directly to its most interesting history, maybe they're worth preserving. If you decide to do some restoration work, consider swapping historically significant parts rather than redoing them. For example, if you get hold of a tired 1950s bobber with custom tank paint like that found on the nose of World War II war planes, keep the faded original as it is and redo the design on a replacement tank. If you redo a bent-up race bike, see about replacing rather than repairing damaged parts, particularly if the bike was owned and crashed by a well-known rider.

A World War II–era Japanese utility trike is an unusual specimen. This 1938 Mazda came from Bud Ekins, the famous Hollywood stuntman and champion off-road racer. He got it from one of the studios, though whether it was used in a movie or for work around the lot is not known. Ekins was interested in antique motorcycles long before they hit collector radar.

Market Value

The value of an unrestored bike has at least two dimensions. One is its dollar value—what some fan of that bike in particular, or of preserved condition generally, would give you for it. That worth is subject to the vagaries of the marketplace. If you have a unique bike that a collector of considerable means is determined to possess, you might get more than the price of your house for it. Of course, most bikes are not that one.

Dollar values are shifting and unpredictable, especially with unrestored bikes because each is unique. Internet searches of auctions and for-sale ads can give you some sense of value. (Look for posting and sale dates, as there is now material on the Internet that is more than a decade old.) It's also critical to learn as much as possible about the particular bike at issue. Who owned it and how and where was it used? How has it been looked after? What sort of documentation comes with it? Are most of the parts original, either as of manufacture or from the time it was customized, raced, featured in some film or event that popularized it?

In addition to books and Internet searches, fellow owners of bikes like yours are an invaluable source of information, as are their motorcycles. If there is a club devoted to your marque or that includes bikes like yours, join it. Its members already possess much of the knowledge you seek. Motorcycle people are usually proud of the bikes they own and happy to speak to others about them, though you may encounter some caution. Recent times have reminded us that there are kooks and swindlers in the world at all income levels; enthusiasts with motorcycles they cherish may want to get to know you a bit before they open their garage or home to you. If it takes time to learn the bike's history and details, it's time well spent. Unrestored fans thrive on history, so what you learn may help reassure potential buyers and make the bike more desirable.

It's also wise to track down and speak to recognized authorities on the bike you own. Their dollar value projections may be helpful, at least in establishing a baseline or range. More important will be their knowledge of which parts the factory fitted. Even on that point, however, there can be differences of opinion. As model years change or supplies of particular parts run short, manufacturers may fit components from a prior year or model that are atypical, yet original, to a given bike nonetheless. A few early 1970 models, for example, might have used up the last of the 1969 tail lenses, or suppliers of one headlight may have met a strike or a materials shortage such that the bike manufacturer switched brands midstream. Generally, the smaller the manufacturer, the more likely there will be differences, but the biggest makers can confront challenges that produce inconsistencies. Even the bike's year of production may be recorded differently on the title and the I.D. plate. This situation has arisen when a dealer titles a slow-selling bike in the year someone buys it, rather than when it was produced.

Personal Value

In so many areas of life, money is a crude substitute for value. What we want from the bike is a more practical assessment of its worth than the amount of cash some hypothetical person might thrust at us. If you bought it to ride to work, the fact that its dry-rotted tires, hard as croquet balls, are the original rubber has a much different value than if you bought it to sit in a row with other cool unrestored bikes to show friends and not ride. In the former instance, you have every incentive to swap them out for something dependable and safe, and in the latter case you have every reason not to.

It's not uncommon to buy a particular used bike because it's in great condition and then have second thoughts about what to do with it

Kawasaki's 650TT has obvious British influences (BSA), yet it's desirable in its own right today. The faded tank suits its age.

because it's so nice and so original. Where the intended use is punishing, like racing or vintage motocross, thrashing some primo barn-find MV Agusta or Husqvarna may be too much to bear. In that situation, the lucky buyer has a couple of options that preserve the bike. If resources permit, clean it up, keep it as is and pick up something less desirable or rougher to prep for competition. Absent the funds to do that, consider selling or trading it to someone who will place a premium on its nice unrestored condition. Before you sell, scope out something rougher or more common that you can easily get into great running shape with the money from the sale. (Use the methods in the previous section to get a good sense of its monetary value.) Maybe the interested buyer has something else to offer in the deal—a person who appreciates it for what it is likely has experience with that type of riding.

Rarity and age are additional factors to consider in determining whether to use or restore a given bike. The longer a bike survives, the more hazards it has opportunity to confront. We expect something 90 years old to show some patina, dings, scratches, fading, and chipping. Interest in the bike's unrestored state will outweigh concern for these imperfections. The same flaws in a 20-year-old Yamaha will count more strongly against it when there are many bikes of the same age and equal originality in better condition.

There's nothing wrong with patina even in a more recent bike, however. With time, deterioration and accidents will reduce its pool of peers. Eventually, it may be as rare and valuable as something from the teens of the twentieth century is today. In the meantime, if it meets your needs, it has personal value.

The valve covers on this BMW R100S no longer match due to a crash by its first owner. The wreck spoiled his interest in the bike, which became a hand-me-down for his college friends. Current owner, Tim O'Keeffe, knows the story and the original owner and has no interest in fitting a second black cover and undoing a part of this tale.

CHAPTER 4

Preserving What You Have

Any sort of bike can be unrestored, a survivor. With its parts and finishes left as its builders applied them, it is a model, a three-dimensional blueprint, of the materials and methods they used. Likewise, in its blemishes and faults, the unrestored bike reflects the manner in which it was ridden, maintained, and stored—treasured or neglected. Paper notes and computer files can retain some of this information, but they cannot convey the full story, the exact size and shape and texture of each attribute. Neither photographs nor the best high-definition video of the bike shot by a professional will capture every detail or show color exactly the way the real item reveals it.

If the bike has lived a charmed life, dodging most of the harm humans and the environment can throw its way, preserving it may be an easy decision. It may even be simple in practice—do nothing!

What about bikes that haven't missed all the bouncing gravel, blazing sun, hard rides, or clumsy pedestrians? Or a bike that doesn't run, or its tank got dented, or the gauges are faded, or the seats or handgrips are split, or the engine's stuck, or a part broke or got lost—is it just as well to restore it?

Along with comprehensive restorations painstakingly planned in advance, there are refurbishing efforts, full and partial, that proceed more or less accidentally as one thing leads to another. The engine is stuck, so the owner plucks it out and puts it on the workbench. Now the frame is more visible. Stare at that a day or two, and it's easy to take some tools over and yank a couple of other parts off of it. Buzz a few bolts on the wire wheel or jet some corrosion off a bracket in the blasting cabinet, and it's off to the races. Perfecting one thing starts a chain reaction that becomes a total restoration.

Although it's in nice unrestored condition overall, this Merkel-powered Napoleon bicycle has a cracked wooden rim up front. Rather than buy a new one, owner Deke Diegal found another period rim that's solid and unrestored. He'll swap in the replacement without refinishing the wood.

Old bikes can certainly last and command admiration without being restored. Take a look at the early bikes featured in Lap II of this book from Thiem, Indian, and Yale. Compared to a modern machine, some of their parts, paint, or plating looks rough. They ooze character, however, and there are collectors—including their owners—who find their present state superior to a brand new bike's eat-lunch-off-it gleam. It's possible to redress problems, preserve, and even use an older bike without restoring it to as-new condition.

If a part is missing or unusable, a replacement from another unrestored bike of the same make and year solves the problem unobtrusively. An appropriate new old stock part, if you can find it, preserves originality too. For rare bikes, a spare or NOS part may be impossible to come by. In that event the same fabrication that would be required to restore it can be done without intensive polishing to make it shine.

Because they are small and easily removed—compared to an automobile—a motorcycle's painted parts often get resprayed when cosmetic problems arise. What if you have an otherwise nice original-paint bike with one gaping flaw, like a spot of bubbled paint where some chemicals dripped, or an unsightly dent from a fallen tool? A talented body and paint shop can make an old-looking repair with some careful planning and trial and error on a test panel. They may need to spray it on thinner and rub each coat to keep it from building up and looking fresh, deep, and lustrous. The original paint formula may also require some adjustment so that it looks like a faded version of itself.

Dents and dings that aren't too severe can be straightened without need for paint through the "paintless dent repair" (PDR) technique. If something fell on your unrestored bike, a PDR expert may be able to make it vanish without messing with the finish. Should the original paint by the dent be cracked, you can fix that with paint formulated and sprayed to look older after the metal is back in the proper shape.

You may have to talk to a few shops to find one that appreciates your goal of an isolated match of imperfection, making it look "just like old." Once they're on board, they can turn their expertise to your purposes, duplicating the effects of wear and fading to suit the rest of the bike. Whether this effort and expense is worth it depends on many factors, most important being your desire to have that never-restored look. Fixing damaged or missing parts with period pieces of comparable condition will be straightforward. Trying to fix an isolated paint or sheet-metal problem and have the repair be old looking and unnoticeable will be more difficult. Of course, if the isolated repair doesn't look right, you can restore the bike at any time. Restoration is always an option; reversing one never is.

What we're talking about here is preserving an authentic look, not trying to cheat someone. As in any market, we can expect rising interest in unrestored bikes to create pressure for more of them. This may encourage some people to mock up originals with pieces from various sources to sell at a survivor premium. The restored-car world is familiar with vehicles cobbled together from authentic bits and pieces and offered for sale as lost rarities, like some heretofore unknown—or long-lost—original Cobra. Let's hope any trickster hustling some fake original factory racer or counterfeit legendary bike, or stamping bogus VIN numbers or producing fraudulent documentation is exposed, prosecuted, and driven from the scene with no honest buyer out a nickel. Scammers are bad for the hobby, sewing distrust and hard feelings where only good will belongs.

The identification numbers on this Vincent's upper frame member and rear frame member match, as they should. An unoriginal bike might look great and run well, but it won't have top value. Learn the details before you buy.

The best defense against trickery is documentation to prove a given bike's authenticity. If you're not well versed on the model in question, and it's something you're buying in part because of the value of its originality, try to bring someone with expertise along when you look at it. Or bring an expert, even if you are one. It never hurts to have a second opinion.

Preserve Form with Function

Vehicles that don't run—and that someone has to start going through anyway—often get restored as repair protocol has the mechanic moving from one system to the next. Yet mechanical repairs can be made without meaningfully altering the bike's finishes and patina. Engines, brakes, gearboxes, and electrical gremlins can all be sorted without polishing everything to a mirror shine or replacing all the wiring. The market places a premium on unrestored bikes that run—and some shows require that bikes be started. An antique engine can be rebuilt internally with its patina left intact.

Owners who like to ride their bikes can follow the same path, cleaning parts and systems and refurbishing nonworking components until they function properly but not refinishing them. If you want to retain the unrestored look but enjoy safe and dependable operation, work toward this goal, discussing it fully with any outside shops you hire. They can do it. Typical repair shops don't restore the cars and motorcycles they work on. Just because a bike is old or rare doesn't mean any other approach is required as long as everybody knows what look, as well as performance, you want in the finished product.

As nice as the rest of this BSA Super Rocket is on the outside, the motor needed some machine work to run as good as it looks. Owner Rick Wyatt fixed a few anomalies to make it run smooth and strong, yet he did not restore the bike.

The engine, so central to the bike's identity and usefulness, is one area where you may not want to be tenacious about originality, internally. A slightly modified motor—with better oiling or bearings or some stronger parts—will preserve itself better than something stock. In the automotive world, unrestored cars running in vintage events frequently have improved rods, pistons, cams, and other parts, even though on the outside the motors are indistinguishable from a silent museum example never fired, never enjoyed.

As fans of unrestored bikes, we should be very tolerant if not encouraging toward unseen internal tweaks that make these machines more enjoyable, practical, and durable. If they never sputter or roar to life, never carry their owners over a rolling stretch of road, for fear feeble old parts will break, unrestored bikes will not win widespread appeal beyond those happy with stationary art.

Even antique motorcycles can be fun to take out on the roads, though this Royal Enfield was not equipped with lighting. Signaling by hand and riding only during daylight hours are modest sacrifices.

Ridden Survivors

Leaving the bike as is has different implications if you plan to ride it. A worn chain and sprockets, weary shocks, dry rotted tires, sticky cables, a rusty, gummy fuel system, dodgy lights, out-of-balance wheels, or clutch, brake, or gearbox problems don't matter much if the point of the bike is to be seen and not heard. No one is suggesting, however, that you leave alone faulty conditions that undermine the motorcycle's ability to run properly and safely when that is your goal.

If you're a knowledgeable wrench turner, go through all the routine maintenance items discussed in the owner's manual or an applicable repair manual and make sure the bike is roadworthy. If you like to ride but are not skillful at or interested in learning repairs and maintenance, take the bike to a respected shop and have them go through it. To be a practical ride, the bike must be able to

- Start, idle, and accelerate smoothly
- Cruise confidently without wobble or other unpredictable behaviors
- Absorb bumps well enough for basic comfort and control
- Stop well
- Shift through and hold all gears
- Illuminate the road for safe night riding
- Display a clear taillight and bright brake light, as appropriate, to trailing traffic. Not all bikes have turn signals; learn safe hand signaling if yours doesn't.

There is collector interest in old, original tires, especially those that were iconic during various racing and motorcross eras. Because rubber tends to harden and have less grip over time and modern compounds are superior, it's better not to ride regularly on old tires. You don't have to throw them away, however. If they're nice looking vintage tires in otherwise good condition fitted to a machine you want to ride, swap on some modern meats that will hold the road and tell the shop you want the old ones back. You may have to pay a fee for them to dispose of the tires otherwise. When you're done riding the bike and want it to be primarily for display, you can swap the cool old tires back and impress the heck out of people who remember that model when it was new.

Some people do this with original seats too. Search around on the Internet, and you will observe that perfect original seats for desirable bikes can fetch hundreds of dollars. The seat is one of the early items to go—ripping—on many classic bikes, and one with a perfect cover is rarer and that much more original and attractive. Funny thing is, the original seats on many bikes aren't even that comfortable, which accounts for manufacturers like Corbin stepping in and becoming popular. Finding something that's better engineered for comfort makes removing a good original seat even easier. Just keep it, so when you retire or sell that bike, you can swap it back. You can always advertise that you're throwing in a good custom seat along with a beautiful original one to heat up the phone lines—as if anything will still be hardwired then—with buyers.

Swapping out old tires is a must for performance riding on street or track. With a low-mileage original bike, however, it's wise to save original rubber for that extra measure of collector appeal. If you want to ride the bike, store the old meats where they won't be in the way of harm—or a spouse who doesn't quite get the concept.

Finally, if the bars vibrate or aren't well positioned for your comfort, you can fit different grips, handlebar weights, or new bars to make the riding enjoyable. Just save the originals (out of your spouse's sight if necessary, to avoid logical questions like, "When are you ever going to use those again?" Must we survivor advocates be clairvoyants too?).

Preservation Standards

Quantifying uniqueness is challenging at best, illogical or oxymoronic at worst. Survivors are appealing because they haven't been redone—because some marks and wear showing history and use remain. Approaching them from the restored-bike perspective, where the fewest flaws lead to the most points, is inherently contradictory. It's the sense of age that makes survivors what they are. For this reason, preserved bikes suit exhibition classes best, where they vie for crowd appeal rather than judges' points.

Generally, shows that display preserved bikes want what the name promises: machines still fitted as they were built. Where repairs were made or parts swapped in, they should be of the appropriate vintage and look, and not be any more polished or well or differently fabricated, than all the other parts. Show organizers can clarify any specific requirements, such as that the bikes be operable, be ridden a few feet, or still bear the original paint applied by the builder. Unrestored bikes have become quite popular, drawing attention and awards over machines whose owners have lavished considerable sums to make them look like new. Recent proof was the unrestored 1908 Indian torpedo-tank racer that took three awards at the Legend of the Motorcycle Concours d'Elegance in Half Moon Bay, California, a century after it was built. The heavily patina-ed track missile won the Preservation Award, the Sculptor's Award, and Best of Show.

In the four-wheeled realm, another approach to unrestored status is the Bloomington Gold Survivor certification program, developed for unrestored Corvettes in 1990. Under this program, Corvettes (initially) were reviewed in specific areas by marque experts who then certified their authentic unrestored condition. That program is expanding to include other marques. Bloomington Gold Survivor certification brings more specifics to the otherwise vague concept of the unrestored car. To

Retro is a common design theme from clothes to bicycles, yet modern goods are seldom made by the manufacturers or countries of old. The signs of age we might call imperfections are also authenticity marks. This 1911 Reading Standard single is the genuine article.

achieve this certification, a car must pass a road test and then demonstrate authentic unrestored condition inside and out. The certification requires that the car be more than 50 percent unrestored and unaltered in at least three of four areas: exterior, interior/trunk, under the hood, and throughout the chassis. In addition, more than 50 percent of the original finishes must retain factory color adequate to serve as models for cars being restored. With unrestored bikes growing in popularity as their horseless carriage counterparts did, we can expect a program like this to develop for motorcycles as well.

Because every unrestored bike is unique, the pleasure it brings its owner and onlookers is its most important characteristic. The growing interest in this area will bring more unrestored motorcycles onto the public stage and encourage owners of these vehicles to keep them much as time has left them. How they are discussed and valued will change, as will the way people repair and maintain them. Still, their preservation will benefit all enthusiasts by keeping alive what the bikes' makers created. These bikes, and the adventures had on them, are our most valuable sources of motorcycle history.

Opportunity will pass
before the determined eye.

LAP 2:
SURVIVOR
TALES

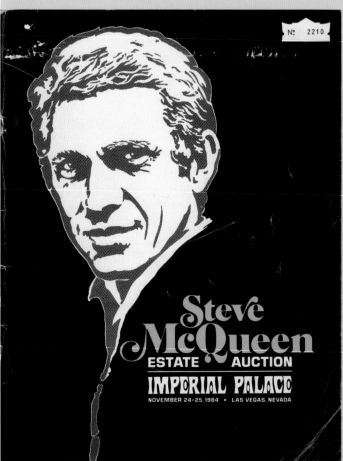

N° 2210

Steve McQueen
ESTATE AUCTION
IMPERIAL PALACE
NOVEMBER 24-25, 1984 • LAS VEGAS, NEVADA

CHAPTER 5

Yesterday's Genius

Pat and Cris Simmons's
1914 Indian Board Track Racer

FAME IS A STRANGE THING, like a suit some people have to wear but don't want to. It's uncomfortable, it stands out, and it has a siphoning effect on the IQs of others who come near. The insightful, clever observations they could make drain away, leaving an empty mind except for a few scattered phrases not used in earnest since fifth grade. "You're great!" an otherwise articulate person might say, and the encounter ends with no one much improved.

Steve McQueen hated that suit. He'd shrug it off every chance he got and reach for transportation from the scene, ideally two-wheeled— but four-wheeled would certainly do and, in time, so would wings. His affinity for the liberation to be had wrestling horsepower and physical laws through a set of steel handlebars and footpegs are well transcribed, as is his fierceness in competing against himself and others. Yet even in quieter moods, he loved the genius behind these inventions. He was most at ease with those who shared such pleasures.

Among them was Bud Ekins, an even more formidable rider than McQueen. A champion rider. Ekins got McQueen more involved with motorcycles and McQueen got Ekins into Hollywood as a stuntman, leading to *The Great Escape* jump for which he was famous. Ekins also had a passion for antique bikes, one the internally combustive McQueen picked up with equal fervor. Both men inspired motorcyclists and collectors.

Pat Simmons met Ekins purely by chance in 1977. Pat and a friend went into the industrial section of Hollywood to look at some old motorcycles. Turned out they were Triumphs, but Pat was hoping to see some domestic bikes. The man with the Triumphs said, "Oh, if you like old American bikes, I should introduce you to the guy across the street,

Steve McQueen entrusted work on his motorcycle collection to Sammy Pierce, whose name is a touchstone for antique bike enthusiasts. Pat Simmons got to visit Pierce and shoot some photos before the McQueen auction broke up and scattered all of the movie great's treasures.

Bud Ekins. He is really into the old American stuff." Pat was aware of Ekins, but at the time, the name didn't click. They headed over.

"Oh, you like old bikes?" Bud asked. He got up and casually walked Pat into a shed. . . . "I was floored," Pat says. Before his eyes, in the most anonymous portion of town, stretched one of the largest and most valuable antique motorcycle collections in the world. It seemed like hundreds. Almost all of them, Bud told him, were pre-1916. Their host was in no hurry. The shop was basically his hobby interest. Bud let his visitors wander around as long as they wanted, jaws hanging open.

Pat had been into motorcycles for about 10 years. He hadn't seen stuff like this, though. Not this old. "I had no idea what I was looking at," he recalls. Motorcycles from this era had disappeared from view, too slow or too valuable for regular use. Bud's collection was a revelation.

"I started to learn," Pat says, "reading like a madman." Works like Stephen Wright's *American Racer*, dumped gas on the fire. "I just flipped out," Pat laughs, "and started going to every antique motorcycle show and auction, and reading every book." He even opened a small shop, Classic Motorcycles of Santa Cruz, where he kept more bikes than he sold.

As the 1970s rode off, McQueen, once an important part of the West Coast bike scene, withdrew from the public eye. Though he had overcome so much adversity, rising from a fatherless and poverty-

After visiting Pierce Cycle, Simmons went to McQueen's hangar to see the rest of his motorcycle collection. Needless to say, there was plenty to fill out a bike fan's wish list.

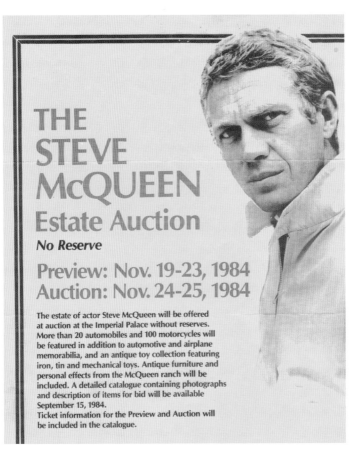

THE STEVE McQUEEN Estate Auction
No Reserve

Preview: Nov. 19-23, 1984
Auction: Nov. 24-25, 1984

The estate of actor Steve McQueen will be offered at auction at the Imperial Palace without reserves. More than 20 automobiles and 100 motorcycles will be featured in addition to automotive and airplane memorabilia, and an antique toy collection featuring iron, tin and mechanical toys. Antique furniture and personal effects from the McQueen ranch will be included. A detailed catalogue containing photographs and description of items for bid will be available September 15, 1984.
Ticket information for the Preview and Auction will be included in the catalogue.

Here's a snap of lot 508 from the pre-auction inspection. The bike behind looks to have been repainted and perhaps fitted with a new tank decal, though the seat leather does not appear restored. There were restored and unrestored examples up for auction.

plagued childhood to become one of the biggest stars of his time, he succumbed to cancer in 1980.

A couple of years later, Pat got a call from another buddy with an intriguing invitation: "I have permission to photograph McQueen's collection—want to go?" "Are you kidding?!" Pat said.

They drove down to Pierce Cycle in Oxnard. Sam Pierce, an old-time ace mechanic, worked on McQueen's vintage bikes. He had lots of them in his shop. "Sam Pierce was so cool," Pat says. "He was in all the old motorcycle magazines—one of these characters in the motorcycle world. He took me through the bikes, and let us just look around." When they asked if they could snap some pictures there, Sam said, "Yeah, go ahead. They're all going to auction."

As they walked around and talked bikes, Pat mentioned that he had a couple of Harleys. Sam quipped, "There's just about enough Harleys in here, we could make a boat anchor, take it out to San Pedro Bay, and drop it." Sam was an Indian man, a former dealer, and that was cool with Pat. In fact, there were a couple of Indian racers there in the shop. As a guy who hit every antique motorcycle event, Pat wouldn't be missing the McQueen sale. He made a mental note to watch for these bikes.

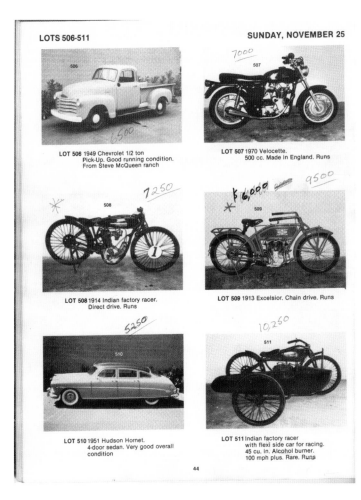

LOTS 506-511   SUNDAY, NOVEMBER 25

7000

LOT 506 1949 Chevrolet 1/2 ton
Pick-Up. Good running condition.
From Steve McQueen ranch

6500

LOT 507 1970 Velocette.
500 cc. Made in England. Runs

7250

LOT 508 1914 Indian factory racer.
Direct drive. Runs

$ 6,000   9500

LOT 509 1913 Excelsior. Chain drive. Runs

5250

LOT 510 1951 Hudson Hornet.
4-door sedan. Very good overall
condition

10,250

LOT 511 Indian factory racer
with flexi side car for racing.
45 cu. in. Alcohol burner.
100 mph plus. Rare. Runs

44

Some catalog notes give a sense of McQueen collection values 25 years ago. It would be nice to come across them for the same money today.

From Sam's, Pat and his buddy headed over to view the rest of the collection, stored in McQueen's hangar at Santa Paula airport. By now, Pat was no stranger to the gorgeous early bikes from so many vanished makers. Yet McQueen's collection pushed things to another level. Near the King of Cool's bi-plane, Pat saw something he'd never seen before: an Indian Chief mail hack. "That totally blew my mind," Pat says. Everywhere they looked were rare, exceptional, and unusual bikes. Soon, fanatical fans and collectors would be vying for them.

The McQueen auction, strategically hosted at the Imperial Palace Hotel in Vegas in fall 1984, was the "it" show for antique motorcycle hounds. Everybody felt that McQueen's best stuff was the best, period, and its connection to the man who embodied rebellion on screen and

What a pleasure to see an antique racer today bearing all the quick fixes its rider made for comfort and necessity almost a century ago. The single-cylinder racer was auctioned in running condition, testament to the Indian's ruggedness.

off added a steely-eyed, steady-handed layer of value no other bikes could attain. Pat thought it could become a feeding frenzy as the day wore on and collectors who hadn't hung in on the bidding early dug deep, determined to leave with some vintage McQueen kit regardless of price.

One of the bikes Pat had seen at Sam's had caught his eye in particular: a single-cylinder Indian board track racer, unrestored, bearing the same paint, scrapes and dings that marked it at the end of its career. Racing in that era, flat-out in high-banked motordromes made of wood, was dangerous, daredevil fare, the sort of thing McQueen would have gone for had he lived in that age. The Indian single even had some sutures—weld marks on the tank and some brazing on the linkage—left just as they were, like lines in an uncompromising face that had known and stared down life's crueler side.

That bike came up in the first lot. Pat couldn't view it well. He was maybe 50 yards back from the auctioneer, but it was in the catalog and he knew it was the one. Once an item starts rolling at auction, it quickly becomes clear which bidders are serious about getting it. Pat stuck to his guns and got the Indian racer. As the show wore on, he picked up a couple of other bikes too. At the time, he felt like he'd spent real money. He's got a different view lately: "By today's prices, they were bargains!"

Linkage is bent and wrapped, but looks are not the driving concern. Note how bicycle-like the frame and fork tubes are. This makes sense, given that Indian, along with many early manufacturers, made bicycles first. Its motorized wares became so successful, however, the company had to farm out its pedal-powered manufacturing.

It doesn't really matter what they're worth. He likes them for what they are—rolling artwork collected by one of his heroes. "I loved Steve McQueen's films, his image," Pat says. "For guys growing up my age who were into motorcycles, we appreciated a guy like that." McQueen respected other bikers and they respected him, both for the characters he played and for his skills as a rider. He was the real deal.

Pat started riding around 1970 when McQueen was at the height of his career. "I was really influenced by two buddies—one loved Japanese bikes; the other loved Harleys." Pat picked a third path and bought a used BSA Victor. It had been apart, but when he put it together and got it running, it was a great little bike. Mainly he rode on the street with friends, but he took it off-road once in a while. "I weighed about 110 pounds soaking wet," Pat laughs. "I was continually getting thrown over the handlebars. . . . When I could afford it I bought a nice Harley in about 1976."

Bikes are a big part of his wife Cris's life too. "She's probably more serious than I am," Pat says. Cris was raised on bikes. Her father had a Honda 750 and she was always his passenger. "Every time he fired that bike up, I'd come running," she says. Her mother scarcely got to ride. Maybe that's why they bought her her own bike, a Yamaha Twin Jet 100, when she was 14 or 15. While any motorcycle sound caught her attention, a particular make seemed to call her by name: Harley-

For a little piece of cardstock, this ticket cost Simmons a lot more than the auction's entry fee. No regrets.

ADMISSION TO ROYAL HALL "C" ONLY

The Steve McQueen

ESTATE AUCTION
NOVEMBER 24 & 25, 1984

IMPERIAL PALACE
HOTEL & CASINO   LAS VEGAS, NEVADA

"C"

Davidson. Her neighbor had a Sportster, and she knew whenever that bike approached. "They have a specific sound," she says. "I can always tell a Sportster."

Cris got into the old school scene early, before there was big money in it. Back then, part of the reason for fixing up bikes with some years on them was that that's what their owners could afford. Cris and her friends learned what car parts would interchange with bikes, like a Delco Remy alternator, to keep repairs cheap. Some people customized bikes as a way to make an older ride special. One guy she knew had a Panhead chopper. He'd often throw her the keys and say, "Take my bike for some exercise."

Not long after Pat stumbled onto Bud Ekins' collection, Cris bought her first Harley—the model with the engine note she always recognized. She's had several since, including an '81 Sturgis she rode to its namesake town in the model's debut year. It was a Harley promotional ride, and she was half a day behind Willie G. on the same mount. Just about every town she rode through, someone would say, "We saw that bike!"

Milwaukee's iron was important enough to Cris that she and a friend started *Harley Women*, the first widely known magazine devoted to women riders. She's been writing and speaking on motorcycles ever since, and just finished a book, *The American Motorcycle Girls 1900–1950* (Parker House, 2009), featuring hundreds of early photographs.

The bikes in those photos are the same extraordinary and mostly extinct makes that Ekins and McQueen found so fascinating. Some might be specific bikes they owned. Motorcycles from the McQueen collection remain special, and Pat's Indian racer is a reminder of his

The back of the tank has been modified or repaired, probably both. In a typical restoration, these lumps and bumps would be cut out, patched, and smoothed over, removing evidence of how race machines actually looked as the stresses of competition took their toll.

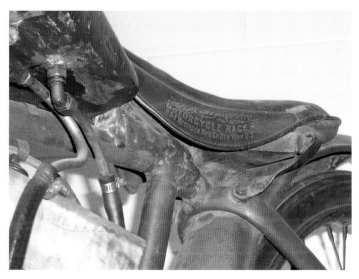

Brazing and more tank work are visible from this angle. By 1914, racing was popular fare, enough for saddle manufacturers to create special models like this Mesinger.

first contact with antique bikes and all the enjoyment he's had learning about and collecting them. "Meeting Bud off the wall like that was one of those things that was meant to be," he says.

They remained friends over the years, and Pat bought a few bikes from Bud. Later, he could have bought a lot more. One day, Bud called and said he was getting out of bikes and was going to sell off his collection. At the time, Pat had other things going on and he let the opportunity slip by.

Pat and Cris Simmons have some wonderful machinery to enjoy today, including Pat's 1928 Indian 101 Scout and Cris's 1934 Harley-Davidson VLD. Steve McQueen and Bud Ekins would approve (and Sammy Pierce would too, by half).

"I'd sell my first born to have those bikes," Pat jokes.

"Is that the son who answered when I called?" I asked.

"No," Pat laughed, "but I'd sell him too."

Pat and Cris do more than collect. They own modern bikes, which they fire up often to reel in a sweeping stretch of sun-dipped road and revel in that V-twin song. They've made a change to their riding gear, though, from previous years. There was no helmet law in California, and the tradition was not to wear one. But Cris figured head protection wasn't a bad idea. Pat's made the adjustment too. "I got a shorty helmet that's really comfortable," he says. With that style, "I don't look like quite as big a nerd."

Motorcycles are a pleasure that never fades, like watching a hero on the silver screen or hanging out with friends, talking about the best things in life.

CHAPTER 6

Dream Chaser

Tom Jones's 1968 BSA Shooting Star
and 1914 Thiem

FRANCE'S ALLURE CAPTURES MANY HEARTS: the poets, painters, writers, chefs, and, of course, guys who collect motorcycles. That's what happened to Tom Jones, 50 years ago, when he read *The Mystery of Mont Saint-Michel*, a Hardy Boys–style adventure set around the ancient island stronghold on the coast of France. The natural wonders and historical intrigue popping off those pages lit a bonfire in Jones's imagination, igniting his own scheme to visit this magical country.

Jones had a friend, Tom H., who read the book too, with equal revelation. France was the place where everything cool, mysterious, and provocative was waiting for those lucky enough to make the discovery and ambitious enough to make the trek.

Inspired and energized, they tackled the necessary logistics for leaving behind Wisconsin's cows and fields and entering the land of wine, women, and wonder. Wine, they knew, was key to France—the beverage of choice and the only thing to sip with the fine French girls populating every city and town. The Toms couldn't drink in the United States, legally, so they had grape soda in wine glasses instead, a simple palate adjustment to remove the fizz and add alcohol later.

When you're 14 and planning a trip to France, you work around your budget, which so far was zero, give or take. It's not too hard to get to the East Coast, so they focused on crossing the Atlantic Ocean, which was messing up their ability to ride all the way there with its deep and sandy bottom, not to mention the whole can't-breathe-underwater issue. Research, including *Holiday Magazine*, indicated that the cheapest way to cross the Atlantic was by Yugoslavian freighter out of New York City. Their destination: Trieste, Italy, on the Adriatic Sea.

A motorcycle sits high on the list of many a boy's dreams. Why not embellish the fantasy with a trip to a land of mystery and romance? Tom Jones aimed high and saw things he will never forget.

Tom Jones collection

Bought in Switzerland, ridden throughout Europe, and now back in the United States for good, Jones's 1968 Shooting Star proved its worth every day. It hauled him and his gear up mountains and across nations—and made 70 miles per gallon doing it.

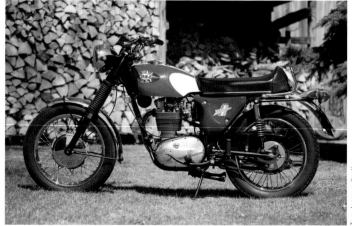

Tom Jones collection

Once in Europe, they would need wheels to travel to and around France. Fortunately, in their voracious reading on the country, they had read warnings about Algerian rebels. Sometimes these rebels would sell scooters to raise money. The scooters were cheap—because they were stolen. For a story designed to discourage would-be buyers of budget transportation, it had the opposite effect.

The teenage boys' plan didn't lose any urgency when Brigitte Bardot started turning up in sultry movie roles in American cinemas. If this is what all French women were like—traffic-stopping blondes oozing sex from every pore—there wasn't a moment to waste. Learning the art of love from women like that would put them on par with the world's great playboys, whoever they were. And they'd have a pretty good story

Jones could draw these decals from memory. They're flaking now beside pin stripes that have faded and polished thin. In other words, they are perfect in a way no restored bike could match.

to start chatting up the girls with, fresh off a Yugoslav freighter aboard stolen motor scooters sourced from Algerian rebels.

Youthful hearts are fickle, though, and other plans and closer young women captured the friends' attention. They got girlfriends at home, and Jones delved into motorcycles. When they graduated from high school, Tom H. went into the Marines and Jones went off to college. France seemed more distant than ever.

Yet Jones didn't forget *The Mystery of Mont Saint-Michel*, or the trip he had dreamed of as a kid. When college ended, he joined the Army and they sent him to Germany, France's next-door neighbor. He still needed wheels for European travels, so he went to the BSA dealership outside Lucerne, Switzerland, and picked out a Shooting Star. It's

Four hundred and forty-one single-carbureted ccs climbing the Alps: The bike's got heart. The author told Jones he'd always liked this model and would be happy to take it off his hands someday. Jones's reply: "That's not going to happen."

Tom Jones collection

a nice looking bike, for one, but he chose it mainly because of its 441cc engine—one-cylinder, one carburetor—something that would be easy and cheap to repair. And it was efficient, making 70 miles per gallon. That was important, for even in 1969, gas prices were high in Europe.

Jones's priority destination was, of course, Mont Saint-Michel, the rocky islet just off the Normandy coast that had sheltered monks and soldiers for a thousand years. He snapped a photo of the Beeser, fully loaded, in the foreground of the island's thirteenth-century monastery, built by King Philip II and called La Merveille, "the Wonder." He'd waited a long time to see those ancient walls jutting up to the sky. The photo was primarily for Tom H., to show him he'd accomplished the major goal of their youth.

A facet of the trip Jones hadn't expected was that he was constantly getting lost, which was strange since he'd brought a map. But the map was part of his childhood dream, one reality was not confined to oblige. The scaled-down drawing he carried came from a book he'd borrowed as a kid to prepare for the big adventure. It was called *French Storybook Grammar* and had been published in 1942. While France's language may evolve slowly, its roads and cities had changed a lot in 27 years.

The bike still displays the same military plate it wore when new. Bet you can remember the license number of the first vehicle to enlarge your world.

And the map didn't bother with some important details for getting around, like road names or numbers.

Being without his friend and a good map were drawbacks on the trip, but riding a new BSA Shooting Star was a cut above the nicked Algerian-scooter plan. The bike was reliable and quickly became his most valuable possession. With nothing but historic cities and scenic countryside beckoning in every direction, Jones made motorcycle touring the focus of his off-duty life.

He'd work extra hours at his Army job whenever he could, to earn comp time, allowing him to take motorcycle trips as long as two or three weeks. On a weekend overnight trip, he would cover 300 to 400 miles. On a three-day pass, he might do a seven-country tour, through countries such as Austria, Lichtenstein, Switzerland, France, Luxembourg, Belgium, and then back to Germany. Once he and the BSA thumper covered 1,000 miles in a day, more than 20 hours in the saddle. Funny, he was never inspired to break that mark.

In his two and a half years overseas, Jones and the Shooting Star visited every country in western Europe. He rode it to North Africa. He rode it to the Arctic Circle. He rode it to the Isle of Man. Together, the American stationed in Germany and his British motorcycle covered more than 50,000 miles.

Although he's been back from the service since the 1970s, Jones hasn't pressed that mileage much farther. He had five motorcycles at home when he left for the Army and has since pushed his collection to

Even books that further dreams have limitations. This map is fine for trying to picture where in a country certain sites are located. It's not much use for actually finding them.

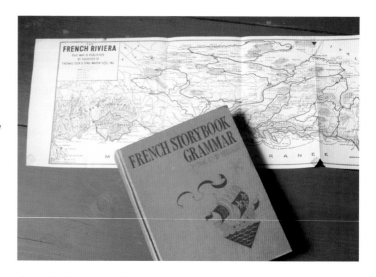

about 75 bikes from 32 different manufacturers. Jones's last long ride on the BSA was to Davenport, Iowa, for an antique motorcycle show. While there, he met a man who "knew BSAs." This "expert" informed Jones that 441s were the worst engine BSA ever made and were "hand grenades waiting to blow up." Riding back to Minneapolis, he thought, "I'm sure glad I didn't know that 50,000 miles ago."

What about the dream of a scooter trip hatched in 1959? To honor that portion of the dream, Jones restored an old Vespa in 1999 and put 5,900 miles on it, including a trip to Sturgis, South Dakota. (In fact, he's made that journey on 30 different bikes, including 7 antique Indians.) His conclusion at the end of the scooter junket: The Shooting Star was the right choice for his European odyssey.

Almost all of Jones's bikes are unrestored and each has a story behind it. One of his favorites is his 1914 Thiem, which may be the only complete V-twin bike from this manufacturer left in the world. It surfaced in 1979, when some high school kids were roving the farm country looking to buy scrap metal. They spied an old iron-wheeled tractor in a field and approached the farmhouse to inquire about buying it. The woman who came to the door let it go for $35.

They boys cut it up, sold the scrap, and went looking for more. Their route brought them back to the same house. They knocked on the door, the same woman answered, and they asked her if she had anything else made of metal that she might want to sell.

The novel-inspired childhood quest was to tour France by motor scooter. A BSA proved better for touring Europe, but Jones made one final nod to his first great scheme by restoring this Vespa and riding it to Sturgis.

She told them that her husband Helmar's motorcycle might still be in the granary but that a tree fell on the building in 1931. The boys went back to the sagging structure and tore off one wall. There, its wheels sunk into the mud, was an antique bicycle-style motorcycle. It had been in that spot unridden, untouched, unknown for almost 50 years. They cut a quick deal and loaded it into their truck.

The boys had seen a lot of old tractors but nothing like this curious bike. They weren't even sure what it was, really, or how old. Seeking any information on what they might have stumbled onto, they drove it over to a motorcycle shop and asked the mechanic to have a look. He told them it was a Thiem motorcycle made in Saint Paul, Minnesota, in

What is believed to be the only complete surviving Thiem V-twin was nearly cut up for scrap by the youths who found it. Instead, they sold it for 30 times their purchase price to a man who knew no better—*or did he?*

the mid-teens of the last century. He also said it wasn't of much interest to him and likely wouldn't be worth much to any collector in the area. If he had stopped right there, the bike might have gone cheap.

The mechanic, a man named Kenny, had met Steve McQueen when the actor-biker came out to a Midwestern motorcycle show. McQueen was interested in the old stuff and wanted unrestored bikes. Kenny told the boys, "Somebody like Steve McQueen, who collects these old museum bikes, might pay $1,000 for something like this." The mechanic took their number in case he could think of anyone else who might be interested, and the two boys left with dollar signs dancing in their heads.

Once they were gone, Kenny thought of his friend Tom Jones, a devout fan of antique bikes and just about anything interesting and two-wheeled. He gave Jones a call and told him about the high school kids driving around with an old Thiem motorcycle in the back of their truck. Jones dialed the lucky youths immediately. He said he wanted to see the bike and arranged to visit the next morning.

Jones had some money saved up for a house project. The house would always be there, though. The Thiem wouldn't. It was going to disappear as quickly as it surfaced; he was sure of it. He put $500 in one pocket, $300 in another, and $200 in a third, and drove to the address

The original starter crank, which spins the back wheel, was still in the toolbox. Note the threaded fittings on the horizontal frame member for adjusting chain tension.

Along with Thiem motorcycles, Joerns Motor Manufacturing Company of St. Paul, Minnesota, built the legendary Cyclone. This V-twin Thiem is on par with the Cyclone for rarity, though the latter's engine was more sophisticated.

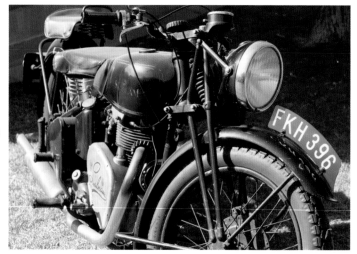

Sunbeam made its high-cam design only one year, 1939, making it a rare bike. Jones bought this 250cc model in Davenport, where it was sold after many years of preservation in a Florida museum.

the boys had given him. The antique V-twin was leaning against the side of the house.

He knocked and a woman came to the door with a spatula in her hand. Jones asked for the two boys. "They're eating their breakfast," she said, and she brought him inside. The house was small and showed its years. As the boys' mother cooked at the stove, the boys told Jones about their plan to try to contact Steve McQueen.

Jones started laying out hundred dollar bills on the kitchen counter. He set down five as eggs and bacon sizzled. Then he set down three more. For a moment, he thought about stopping, reasonably sure he could cut a deal. But when the boys said they'd heard the bike might be worth as much as a thousand dollars, he threw down the last two hundreds. "I have a thousand dollars here," Tom said. "I don't think McQueen is going to come to Minnesota for this bike, but I'll buy it right now."

Before the boys could move, their mother stepped over—grease dripping from the spatula—and scooped up the cash. "Mister," she said, "you just bought yourself a motorcycle. Those boys have never seen a thousand dollars."

Jones had come in a pickup truck and one boy helped him load up his purchase. As they moved the old Thiem around, the youthful seller had a smile on his face—kind of a smirk. Finally, the boy chuckled a little. "What's so funny?" Jones asked him. "Know what we paid for this?" he asked. "Thirty-five dollars."

Several Indians are in the collection, including this 1948 Chief. It went to Sturgis in 1988, one of seven Indians Jones has ridden there.

A few cables are incomplete on the Thiem and the original drive chain was damaged beyond repair. Jones could make it run, though. He's brought far rougher vehicles back to life and the roadways.

Not too many transactions go down where each side is convinced he got a steal. A grand was a lot of money to some rural kids in 1979, but Jones had no regrets. And he's been happier and happier every year as collector bike prices have climbed and climbed, particularly for rare bikes and even more so for ones that are complete and unrestored.

It isn't about the money, though. Neither is Jones. Mostly, he's pleased that a rare machine from early in the motorcycle era surfaced briefly, and he was able to scoop it up, to preserve it and treasure it before it disappeared, perhaps forever. Kenny may have caused him to pay top dollar for the Thiem. On the other hand, had the mechanic called it junk, the boys may have cut it up with a torch.

Today, the Thiem resides in Jones's shop beneath his sword collection and beside a nice Model A Ford. There are other motorcycles in there—some regulars, some just in for work. The Shooting Star is in another building with dozens of additional bikes. All get worked on from time to time, and most see a few miles. More travel awaits those that have not yet gone to Sturgis.

All of Jones's bikes get preserved, spared from the elements and the wrecking yard, and kept intact for future adventures.

Before the first Berghoff
International could be raced, it
had to be broken in. Lee Berghoff
set off on a long trip on the new
Norton, during which this favorite
family photo of him was taken.

CHAPTER 7

International Hunter

Gene Berghoff's 1949 International Norton,
1938 Velocette, and 1969 Honda Dream

THE MEN IN GENE BERGHOFF'S FAMILY have loved motor vehicles since they were a curiosity—one some people thought might not catch on. His grandfather joined the fledgling Ford Motor Company in 1906 when the corporation had only a small group of employees. Maybe that's why Gene's father had no interest in Ford products or those of any other Detroit manufacturer. The bikes and cars that most caught his eye came from Britain, a taste he passed on to his son.

Yet which country's vehicles they prefer isn't the outstanding Berghoff trait. More definitive is their skill and tenacity in making motorcycle schemes come true. What his father wanted, he found a way to get, be it a rare bike or an improbable plan for one. So it is with Gene. He thrives on cool motorcycles and their histories, and he's relentless at gathering both.

One of his favorite possessions is his 1949 International Norton, a genuine factory race bike. A DVD on Norton's history features this very bike running around the Isle of Man. His father had one decades earlier, when the bikes were new, and it's mere coincidence—or providence—that the one Gene hunted down is from the same year.

Norton's International is a seldom seen bike and rare in the United States. The factory made a very limited number of International Nortons over its production run and didn't schedule any of them for U.S. export. Those now here were brought across the Atlantic individually by determined enthusiasts. Gene's father wrangled one into the country for a high purpose: racing. Only the Manx was faster, and they had much in common, with comparable capabilities once he uprated the International with alloy and high-performance parts.

Gene Berghoff's father, Lee, sponsored a 1949 International Norton on racetracks in Detroit and beyond when the bike was new. The one Berghoff hounded down decades later also happens to be a '49.

Despite his efforts, Gene's father never lined up on a racetrack starting line with his International Norton. He didn't want to. He'd brought the Norton over and reworked it for another rider with a gift for speed. That man's name was Brooks, and he was a well-known black motorcycle racer in Detroit. People came from miles away to watch him. He was slow off the line—a fault of his bike, but his abilities and nerve carried him to the front.

Gene's father admired Brooks's riding and offered him a partnership. He would buy a bike that was fast off the line, and everywhere else, and Brooks would ride it. They'd share the prize money. Brooks accepted. Gene's father contacted England, bought the desired Norton, and had it shipped over, then wrenched it up to hi-po specs. The first weekend he had it, he rode 2,000 miles to break it in quick and get it into Brooks's capable hands. The Brooks-Berghoff partnership was a

The International has an attractive engine topped by the factory's "hairpin" valve springs, which were designed for quick replacement on the racetrack.

terror on the track, with many wins. Both Brooks and the race-tuned International were as fast as Gene's father had believed.

If fielding a never-exported Norton on a Detroit racetrack was unusual, so was taking your Indian motorcycle overseas, compliments of the U.S. Navy. Gene's father pulled that off too. After the Korean War, he was scheduled for deployment to the Mediterranean. Nice country, he thought, and he wanted to explore it on two wheels. His captain was a friend from the war, and as always Gene's father was not shy about asking for what he wanted. Instead of trying to sneak it aboard, the captain had a better idea: "Paint it battleship gray," he said, "and they'll

Given its age, this Norton is very clean. The marks that distinguish a bike this well preserved from a restored example are subtle, like plating on an important bolt displaced from wrench contact or a soft surface like the Roadholder badge polished by cable movement.

think the Navy owns it. When we reach port, I'll 'consign it' to you." As a child, Gene saw a photograph memorializing this trick—his father's Indian in gray paint strapped to the railing of a Navy destroyer.

When it was his time to get into cars and bikes, Gene followed his father's lead. He has an Indian of his own, as well as British cars and motorcycles. He's restored a number of XKEs, his father's favorite way around on four wheels. The elder Berghoff was head of large company and received a new car regularly as part of his compensation. He always gave that one to his wife and kept driving his XKE. He would even put chains on the tires and drive it through Minnesota's frigid, snowy winters.

Father and son have much in common, yet they didn't get to do many projects together when Gene was young because his father was busy working. Later in life, Gene asked his father if he wanted to collaborate on restoring an old bike. His father said yes.

"What kind?" Gene asked.

"How about an International Norton?"

Gene had never heard of an International Norton, so his father shared the story of the bike he bought from the factory.

Excited to find a machine like the Detroit race bike, Gene started dialing motorcycle shops in all the major cities, asking if any of them had a line on what was basically the street version of the ferocious Norton Manx. A few people did. The bikes were apart, though basket cases. And they were not cheap.

As hard as he hunts to find the bikes he wants, Berghoff is just as interested in their histories. He researches the background on most every bike he buys and has made good friends among their prior owners.

When Berghoff told his father they could get a torn-apart bike for five or six thousand dollars, his father balked. He didn't think they were worth that much money, especially in pieces. Instead, Gene's father decided to make a sculpture of his old racing-partnership bike. Gene's friend, Vincent mechanic and Bonneville record holder Steve Hamel, actually had an International Norton, though not for sale. He let Gene's father take all the measurements he wanted, from which the elder Berghoff created his artistic rendition.

Gene enjoys the sculpture and his dad's artistry, but he wasn't done chasing the elusive Norton. Years later, after his father passed away, he

This 1938 Velocette was not among Berghoff's motorcycle quarry. Yet it was in such excellent original condition, and so reasonably priced, he couldn't pass it up.

decided to track one down for his collection. Thus began a years-long odyssey of search and call, search and call. Every time Gene got wind of an International, he'd run it by Steve Hamel. If Hamel didn't approve it, he let it go.

Five years into his search, Gene found a small ad for an International in a British magazine. He rang the seller and learned that the bike was mostly original, except that the engine had been rebuilt. Hamel had told him these engines were challenging to rebuild and that it had to be done right or the bike wasn't worth buying. Gene told the seller he was interested, but before he sent the money he wanted the engine's rebuilder to speak to Hamel. The seller agreed—yet the verifying conversation proved hard to set up. The engine builder was busy and hard to reach, and Hamel was tied up too, mostly modifying Vincents. When the two experts finally talked, all reservations vanished. The British machinist knew his Norton engines, and he had done everything Hamel thought necessary.

The following day, Gene called the seller with words he'd waited a long time to say: The bike is sold. Unexpectedly, that's what the seller told him. While the machinists played phone tag across the Atlantic, another buyer had walked in and bought the coveted Norton. Gene was stunned and dismayed. He had put a half-decade into this quest, and thought about it long before, hearing stories from his father from the Brooks racing days. He decided that it wasn't his timing that was

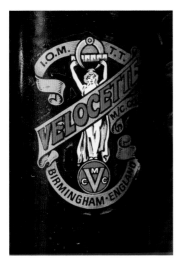

It's hard to assess all of the characteristics that make a bike appealing. Reliability and performance are factors, of course, but there are intangibles, too: the style and artistry throughout. A perfect original decal like this is one more thing to study and admire.

If it's a bike you'd like to run, evidence of mechanical condition is important. Here's a place where meaningful wear is reassuring. Over the decades, this oil filler cap has been spun off and refitted many, many times.

wrong. It was the sale. That bike was meant to be his, and he was going to chase it right to the buyer's door.

With some prodding, the seller gave him the man's name and soon Gene was listening to Britain's distinctive ring-tone. A man's voice answered, and Gene said, "You have my bike." He offered the man 50 percent more than he'd paid, but the Englishman declined. Before he hung up, Gene asked him to do something. "Write that number on a piece of paper and put it on the ceiling over your bed so that it's the last thing you see before you shut your eyes at night. Hopefully, you'll dream about it (or have nightmares) all night long, and by morning you'll be convinced the right thing to do is to sell it to me."

Two days later, the man who scooped him on the International gave Gene a call. "It's your bike," he said. Gene sent the money, and the man arranged for the second International Norton to be shipped from England to this American family. A '49 Norton International like the one his father fielded on Michigan racetracks some 60 years ago is a special bike for Gene.

He has another beautiful English survivor, a 1938 Velocette. Virtually every nut, bolt, washer, and screw is the one that came on it new. It's also one of the few bikes Gene has acquired that he initially had no plan to buy. He'd even seen it in a British magazine a month before the vintage motorcycle auction in Saint Paul, Minnesota. A British dealer brought it over for that event.

An original seat is rare
even on motorcycles
40 or 50 years newer
than this one.

Gene goes to several auctions a year and always has a short list of things he wants. This bike wasn't on it. Yet once at the venue for Saint Paul's event, Gene discovered that his motorcycling friends saw a lot more to the Velocette than he did. They couldn't stop gawking at it and marveling at how little the bike had been messed with in 65 years.

The Velocette came up for bid in the afternoon, after many of the visitors had already bought and gone home. The magazine he'd seen it in the previous month had valued it at $12,000, but at the auction, bidding started to die at $6,500. Gene's friend Randy Baxter, of Iowa's Baxter Cycle, began nudging him. Suddenly the pre-war Velo was looking good. When the gavel fell, he owned it.

Although he doesn't do his own engine work, Gene does keep his bikes looking immaculate. He took the Velocette home and spent 10 hours cleaning it. What he didn't do was fire it up, but he'd kicked the starter and knew the engine was free. Because he has other bikes, it was two years before he got around to starting the Velocette—or trying to. This time, when he put his foot on the kick starter, it wouldn't budge. Something had seized.

He took the bike to a motorcycle shop, which opened up the case. Turns out, not everything was original. The prior owner had spruced up the internals, fitting new rings and pistons. Never run much, the fresh parts weren't embedded with oil the way well used ones are. Some moisture had gotten in and seized the rings to the cylinder walls.

Berghoff's 1966 Honda Dream was another machine too good to pass up. The tires are original and the saddlebags are still stuffed with period newspapers to hold their shape.

Actual miles…

In about two hours, the shop had the Velocette running. Now the bike starts and runs as beautifully as it looks.

Gene isn't rabid about unrestored condition. Mainly, he likes nice bikes. When something is unrestored and in great shape, however, he'll leave well enough alone. Like the Velocette, his 1966 Honda Dream is remarkably well preserved, with only 2,000 miles, the same number his father put on the International Norton its first weekend. The newspaper that the original owner stuffed in the Dream's saddle bags to hold their shape is still there. The pages are dated 1970.

Gene loves to collect, and he gathers as much history on each bike as he can—prior owner's names, things they did with the bike, pictures if he can get them. He has met every owner of his restored 1938 Indian and family members of the man who bought it new. He even had a party and got all those people together at his home to share photos and stories and to sign a picture of the motorcycle they knew like family.

The bikes that are dearest to him will be around for a long time. Yet Gene isn't a collector who only accumulates. "My rule is this," he says. "I have so much space. Anytime I buy one, I sell one." Given Gene's tastes, and the polishing and tuning he and Hamel do, a lucky buyer can get a pretty nice machine. If the tire is on the other wheel, and you're the one with a bike that Gene is set on acquiring, look out! History shows that when this family charts a particular path, for a particular motorcycle, odds are good that that's exactly what is going to happen.

There are handlebars and a seat, true.
Yet, at its essence, a motorcycle is
an engine between two wheels.

WIDE OPEN
THROTTLE

If a typical worker makes a mistake seated at his job he will likely not be thrown into a fence or have a half-dozen co-workers pile on top of him. This is why dirt track racers often transition to other occupations. Before he transitioned, Denny Kannenberg, number 20, enjoyed a lot of time riding in this position.

CHAPTER 8

Beyond the Bone Yard

Kannenberg/Bones Flat Track and Lo-mi Treats

THE BONE YARD IS A QUIET CONVOCATION, where the quick and the crumpled, the tired and the worn, commune. Wherever the road goes, they have gone. Whatever speed you have traveled, they have traveled. In every hulk, from the rusted and twisted, plundered and spare, to the freshest arrivals a few parts and a few hours from life's crackle and whine, there is a story. These bikes have carried thousands of riders millions of miles.

When you walk the rows of a motorcycle bone yard, what you see depends on what you're looking for and how your mind works. A dreamer could waste endless days and dollars here. A pragmatist could keep himself in cheap transportation for life.

Denny Kannenberg did not come to motorcycles through salvage. He's a dirt rider, a flat-tracker. He wore out bikes one at a time, on his own. The wrecking yard was a post-racing career, something to keep the dollars flowing when the years under the lights, before the crowds, jamming away half-sideways with one hot shoe skimming the sod and a swarm of angry pursuers buzzing in his ears, were over. Motorcycle salvage fed his family, then absorbed it.

Denny started racing in the 1950s. His high school was one of the largest in the nation, yet in a class of 630, only 6 rode motorcycles. There were more bikers in the area, though, and Denny found them. He joined the Sioux Falls Cycle Club, and in 1958 got his first taste of racing. The club held a winter dash up the Big Sioux River—on it, not beside it.

They lined up near downtown, some 50 riders across, and raced north to Baltic, South Dakota. Half of them crashed in the first bend. Not Denny. The narrowest line divides fast from too fast and Denny

A mechanical failure split the engine cases, which Kannenberg sold off. Many years later a friend bought them and now they're back with the bike they were made for.

Harley-Davidson's mighty KR was a sensation in the dirt. Kannenberg bought this one from West Coast builder Floyd Emde, a former winner of the Daytona 200.

could find it and hold it. As the rest of the pack wiped out and fell behind, he was the first man to Baltic. First rider, anyway. He was 14.

His parents weren't crazy about a motorcycle-racing son, but he loved it. They figured a teenager could get caught up in worse things. Denny bought a pickup truck to haul his bike around and threw in with the flat-track crowd. He worked his way up through South Dakota's competition, then decided to go east to the "big city," Minneapolis, to see how far this passion might take him. Among a bigger, better funded pool, he expected to be outclassed or at least outpaced. It didn't play like that, though. His years riding trails and shooting hills had served him well.

In the early 1960s, in a sport where sponsorships were rare, Denny landed one. Kenny DeGonda, owner of Honda Town in Minneapolis, was looking to call attention to his bikes and his dealership. A racer pulling laps at the front could do that. At a time when Triumphs, Nortons, and BSAs clogged the leader boards, Denny rode a Honda—a pilgrim from the land of the rising sun.

Sold to a drag racer but now back in the family, the old 450 flat tracker still has its Honda 125 racer tachometer.

Honda dealer sponsorship had some perks, like the first 450 engine in Minneapolis. When this bike was running right, which was often, it foreshadowed a more sweeping end to the British motorcycle empire.

In 1966, DeGonda got the first 450 Honda in Minneapolis and he dialed Denny the moment it arrived. They pulled the hot dual-overhead cam bike out of the crate and started wrenching it into a flat tracker. They lengthened the swingarm, fitted Amal carbs, open megaphones, and some other trick parts and packed up for a race in Wausau, Wisconsin. Denny remembers *Hot Rod* magazine featuring the 450 engine on its cover. The hoopla was justified: Denny beat the field in the bike's debut race.

They headed for the next event, but when they unloaded, the race-winning Honda refused to fire. Denny cracked the gas cap and found out why. There wasn't a drop of liquid in it and none in the float bowls either. The win in Wausau came precisely at the end of the fuel. In racing, luck is as important as skill.

That 450 was good for many wins. It would pull strong to 10,000 rpm—so high Denny used a tach from a 125 Honda road racer. He didn't sell that bike until after he retired. It went to a drag racer friend, who put his own miles on it, a quarter at a time.

Look quick: Getting this shot is the longest this family has sat still on motorcycles. Between them, Kari, Denny, Kim, and John could spec out, tear down, rebuild, and ride these bikes over serious terrain. There's a library's worth of motorcycle know-how here.

Denny had another favorite ride before that, a Harley KR he bought out of *Cycle News* in 1964. The bike belonged to Floyd Emde, Harley dealer and Daytona 200 winner. It was advertised as ready to race. Denny sent $600, and they shipped the bike from California. He uncrated it, fired it up, and got all the way to second gear before putting a rod through the front cylinder. Pulling it apart, he found his "ready to race" Harley was more aptly "already raced"—a lot. If this bike was going to carry him to a win, the motor needed some new life.

Denny was flying out to a race at Ascot Park, just south of Los Angeles. He took the KR motor apart and distributed pieces between his carry-on baggage and his suitcase, sneaking it west without a shipping charge. Once in California, he entrusted it to super-tuner Jerry Branch, who was building some of the fastest bikes in the country. Branch worked his magic and shipped it back, for $750. He passed on some speed tricks, too, such as running automatic transmission fluid in the gearbox and lapping the valves every five races. Denny bolted the super-tuned twin into the frame, took it to a race in Elkhorn, Wisconsin, and ran fast time for juniors.

"Adrenaline is the greatest drug in the world," he says, but racing's a dangerous source for it. When you're running a hard-tail motorcycle into corners at 100 miles an hour with all of a helmet and leathers separating you from dirt and fences going 0, the party stops as abruptly as you do. Entering a race in Lincoln, Illinois, Denny was among the

"Hello, do you have used motorcycles?" "Hold on a minute— let me take a look around…. Yes, we do."

top juniors in the nation in points. At full scream, luck took a pit stop and bikes tangled and tumbled, collecting Denny in the snarl. The crash snapped his leg and finished the best season in his career early. He broke his leg a couple of times over the years, with a collar bone and some other human chassis parts thrown in.

His wife, Kari, tolerated racing, but daughter Kim was the swing vote. She was a supporter at first and even wheeled her little bicycle to the starting line to join daddy once, only to have race officials cry foul. If that's the way it was going to be—no three-year-olds, motorized vehicles only—there was nothing to do but protest the system. Her mostly civil disobedience won out, and Denny hung up his metal shoe.

That's how he and Kari characterize his retirement when they want to razz their only child, but Denny knew racing is an early life endeavor. He took his last win near the site of his first, at the Sioux Empire State Fair, at age 27. There was a new goal now. As Denny puts it, "I had to find a way to make a living without getting a job." Awash in trophies, photos, bikes, and bits, it didn't take much soul-searching to find his field of interest.

In 1971, he started his first shop fixing motorcycles and selling parts in the Twin Cities. They moved mostly British stuff early on, changing as the market did. As that went well, he opened a salvage yard on three acres in Jordan, Minnesota, in 1976. Four years later,

Spend decades in the motorcycle business and you'll encounter all sorts of neat ways to motorize a two-wheeled vehicle. This tot of a minibike sports McCulloch chainsaw-engine power.

he started a shop in a third town, Bloomington, Minnesota, selling supplies and accessories.

For a time, he, Kari, and their employees operated all three stores. Kari, who left a corporate job to join the motorcycle biz, did the books for all locations, traveling 150 miles a day to balance the till at each address. Eventually they sold the outlet store, letting the repair shop go a few years later. The big operation by then was salvage.

The 3 acres in Jordan filled up, so they bought a 10-acre plot in the same town. In 1999, they moved thousands of motorcycles a few minutes north on Highway 169. Today, total inventory runs about 10,000 bikes. In nearly four decades in the salvage business, the family has seen almost every kind of motorcycle, including a few wayward bikes of Denny's that have found their way home.

Years after he sold it, Denny's first-in-the-state Honda 450 was offered back to him. He bought it on the spot. More remarkable were his original Harley engine cases, which he'd sold out of his shop, needing repair, around 1973. A year ago, a friend called to say he'd just bought some old KR cases that the seller thought once belonged to Denny Kannenberg. "Are they 54KR2443?" Denny asked. He'd had to write that number before every race. They were, and are, and now they're back in Denny's hands, along with the rest of the bike and the California title with Floyd Emde's name on it.

The Go-Devil is another take on the space-conscious minibike idea. It starts out like this . . . and folds down to this. They were a popular carry-along in a car or private plane—something for entertainment or local transportation at your destination.

In order to race their 750 flat trackers, BSA had to build a minimum of 200 bikes for the street. This is one of the A70 Lightnings produced for that purpose.

In addition to bikes with family history, they have tucked away many rare and low-mileage motorcycles for their own collection.

Today, Kim runs much of the day-to-day salvage business with plenty of support and help from her husband, John Bones. The former race protester doesn't oppose riding, far from it. Kim's been kicking up dirt since she was a little kid, beginning on a Honda MR50 and progressing to a Yamaha DT100 and MX175, Honda XL350, and then a Kawasaki KX125 that John hopped up with a KDX 200 air-cooled motor. Lately she rides the same bike as her dad, a Yamaha TT-R 230.

Kim and John sell motorcycles and parts by day, and ride on weekends and vacations. They first met on bikes on a South Dakota trail—John was going downhill and Kim was going up, riding her friend Larry's Kawasaki KX500. John caught one look at the rider

BSA's 750 flat tracker, homologated by the A70 Lightning pictured previously. The engine is the most obvious similarity. This one was shipped to the United States for Kannenberg, but he switched over to a Triumph. Because this bike was built for him, he acquired it later.

A family friend from Iowa bought this 1948 Indian flat-tracker to vintage race. Kannenberg had had a 648 Big Base a few years earlier and picked up this modified 45-cubic inch street version for its similarity to that bike. They are beautiful machines with an exciting history.

and the bike and thought, "Wow, that's the girl for me!" Later, when Larry joined the Kannenbergs for a week-long snowmobiling trip, he brought John. "He started calling after that," Kim says. These days they ride trails with their kids—Johnny, Kelli, and Dustin—and sometimes with Denny and Kari too.

You don't win races, or a dirt-riding girl, without a competitive streak, so naturally Denny and John sometimes push each other. Denny returned to the track for a little vintage racing, and how could John, a dirt rider his whole life, pass up something like that? At the 50th Sturgis rally in 1990, the family took out four or five truckloads worth of merchandise to sell, but the track was too much for Denny to resist—so was the prospect of running some laps with John.

This four-cylinder Indian with a factory sidecar is said to have been on the assembly line when the Japanese bombed Pearl Harbor, making it one of the company's last prewar bikes. Paint may be an older respray.

Denny knew the event promoter well, so they set up a three-mile "grudge match" between father and son-in-law on the old Sturgis half mile. John was running a Shell Thuet Yamaha and Denny had a classic Triumph, both 750s. "I didn't really know what was going on in John's head," Denny says. "We take off and I realize, 'Hey, he's serious about this, running into the corner real hard.'" For five and three-quarter laps youth held experience at bay, but Denny was back in the points race, running on instinct. His Triumph transformed into his old 450 or his hot-shot KR. He came out of the last turn in the draft, swung wide, and took the win in the closing feet. The crowd went nuts.

John missed the win there, but he's had other fine moments on two wheels. One special trip was a Baja ride with tuners and management from the Kawasaki factory team—Randy Hall, Roy Turner, Rick Ash, Brett Leef—plus some top Baja riders such as Max Switzer and Tim Smith. A dozen of them rode 670 miles in three days, blasting over the loose stuff wide open to stay on top of it. John especially enjoyed following Switzer, whose head and shoulders stayed perfectly still as his bike pounded over the terrain. John started with a new-in-the-crate Kawasaki KX, and by the end of the ride it was basically junk—sand, knocks, and dings all over. The trip was worth it.

As Denny and Kari ease up on the business side, Kim and John press on. There will be more adventures with family, friends, and legends, past and future. New bikes will come and go, adding tales of their own—maybe one of yours.

The Hamel Harley has been in the family since new in 1948. It has never been restored, and there is no plan to do so.

There is little doubt Steve Hamel could draw this speedometer in perfect detail from memory or sit on the bike with his eyes closed and bring his fingers down directly onto the gas caps, hand-holds for his first motorcycle rides.

CHAPTER 9

Flat-earth Scientist

Steve Hamel's British and Italian Hot Rod Bikes

WHOOSHING AIR, THUNDERING PIPES, intoxicating fumes swirling around you as your father's Panhead chases down distant barns and steeples, his powerful hands guiding the bars as you cling to the gas caps reveling in a vibrant, sensory chaos. Shape your worldview with memories like these and a desk job won't fire your engine.

Steve Hamel spent his favorite youthful moments charging the wind on his father Mel's 1948 Harley. Moving and motorcycling has defined him ever since. From rider to dealer to scientist of speed, Hamel chases his dreams at wide-open throttle. Ensconced in his machine shop, measuring, milling, sleuthing, and strategizing, he plumbs predecessors' deeds and quick peers' minds for a few extra horsepower, a couple more miles more per hour. In off-duty hours, he collects motorcycles that speak to his soul.

Most of Hamel's recent work involves his quest to be fastest on the Utah salt. His mount is the venerable Vincent—the marque that built its name on speed. The year Mel's Panhead came out of Milwaukee, Rollie Free went to Bonneville and beat 100 by half on the black steed from Stevenage. Free laid full out, arms and legs outstretched, his weight balanced on the seat to maximize drive-wheel traction. For aerodynamics, he wore a bathing suit and sand shoes, though he tried full leathers first. They ballooned and ripped in a run that peaked at 148. Being so close, he wasn't going to give up. According to Hamel, who has deeply delved into this history, Free had swim trunks on. He borrowed some oversize tennis shoes and ended up wearing his wife's shower/swimming cap. Some photos show him wearing a helmet, but Hamel says Free ditched it before he made his run.

Speedy bikes often see a little tweaking and tuning as the years run by. The Duc has aluminum clips-ons here (originals were steel) and non-original hand-grips. Mods are few and don't harm the bike's enormous street appeal.

The speedster in a Speedo blew records and bystanders away. His superhuman feat was undiminished when Hamel learned of it decades later. Hamel bought his first Vincent in 1979, step one in a plan to beat Free and the riders who followed. There were other fires to attend to, though, like making a living and raising a family.

For a base camp, Hamel opened a motorcycle shop—Sterling Cycle Works—selling and fixing the machine that defines him. While he laughs today that the shop made no money, he kept food on the table. Running a bike business sharpened his skills and brought other spirited souls into his life. The Sterling Cycle days also put Hamel onto some rare and sexy motorcycles, bikes he holds and preserves for their value to him, not the marketplace.

One shop regular was Kathy Grant, member of the Central Racing Association. She helped run a shop called Roseth Racing, an ideal job to support a track habit. Grant found her race form on a 250 Suzuki and 350 Yamaha, graduating to a Suzuki 450 and finally a 500 Kawasaki. She raced at Daytona, Road America, Blackhawk, Mid-Ohio, Gimli (Manitoba), and elsewhere and did street racing in Steamboat Springs. There were few women competitors, so Grant mixed it up with the boys from 1977 to 1988. Career highlights include a pole position in the national amateur races at Daytona.

Though her race points came on Japanese bikes, she was always enamored of the Italian breeds. When a Roseth customer wanted to

Here's the 750 early in its life with racer Kathy Grant aboard. The pictured seat has had a section cut out of it—perhaps to accommodate a second rider or allow an even flatter riding position—and uses a snap-on seat cover. Also, the rear fender is not fitted (compare previous photo).

deal on his '75 Ducati 750, Grant pounced. "I rode it around town and back and forth to work," she says, noting that, if anything, it was the bike that belonged on the track.

A Ducati Sport is, in only slightly biased eyes, one of the more seductive bikes ever built. If anyone's making something much sexier, they haven't shipped it to earth. Hamel wanted that bike, and he let Grant know it. When it was time to move on, she considered no other buyer. "I knew it would be in good hands with Steve," she says.

Another Italian twin Hamel absorbed through the shop is his '72 Moto Guzzi V-7 Sport. He's had three V-7s over the years, and for a time he owned all of them at once. "They defined an era," he says. "They're drop-dead gorgeous with performance—long-legged high-speed cruising, . . . really fun to ride." This bike was posted for sale, virtually new, on the shop bulletin board. The ad sat and sat until finally the owner pulled the posting. When Hamel called and offered to buy the pretty Guzzi, the man said he had decided to keep it.

Hamel told him he'd call again, and he did, for more than a decade, waiting for a change of heart. After 11 years, a mutual friend contacted him. "I think it's time," the friend said. Hamel called the one-time seller and, sure enough, it was time. When Hamel bought it in 1983, the V-7 had 2,700 miles on it. It still has less than 5,000, retaining such an uncorrupted original feel that author Greg Field featured it in his book, *Moto Guzzi Big Twins* (MBI Publishing, 1998).

Little touches count. Ducati designers ran the cooling fins lengthwise on the forward cylinder, side-to-side on the rear, to make them parallel. This arrangement aids airflow.

Along with Italy's curvy fare, Hamel has a soft spot for British makes, and not just Vincents. His Norton International is a third survivor gem to come from his cycle-business days. The customer here was a Brit named Bishop, an aircraft engineer living and working in the United States. He brought from England the International he had purchased there in 1969. As the years passed, however, he seldom had time to ride it, and eventually, with its kick start and antiquated manners, the old Norton became more than he could manage. He told Hamel he wanted something that was easier to ride. When Hamel offered him a Mark III Commando, the Nortons traded homes.

With a little cleaning up, the International fired and ran so well Hamel rode it to Sturgis, South Dakota, in 1994. His father, Mel, took an R75/5 BMW and several friends joined them for the trip. Cruising at 70 miles per hour, the antique stayed on the bit, keeping pace with the modern bikes. By their halfway point—Wessington Springs, South Dakota—however, the International's engine started to complain. The protestations grew louder all the way to Sturgis.

The problem was castor-oil, the old-style lubricant on which the ex-British performance bike had been maintained. It's quite effective, Hamel says. Fighter planes used it in World War II, but that's when the "bean oil" hasn't gone rancid. Sitting so long in the Norton's crank case, the organic liquid had decomposed, corrupting the engine's bottom

Original shark-gill exhaust components from Silentium in Torino, Italy, are hard to come by today. As with virtually everything on this V-7, these are factory-fitted pieces.

The long, low, and solid stance suggests pleasant highway cruising. Paint is original and looks great having never been stored outside.

end. Rather than risk blowing it up, Hamel shipped the Norton back from Sturgis. The motor is on his projects list for a rebuild, though the bike's originality, including finishes, will not be disturbed.

Perhaps Hamel's favorite unrestored bike is one he picked up before opening his own shop. Freaky Fred's Shade Tree Engineering was a garage that did tuning and repairs. Among the commonplace bikes that came and went was a rarer machine that stayed: a Seeley-framed Matchless G50. The 1970 Seeley went to Freaky Fred's for some difficult engine work, fitting a new cylinder. Before it was finished, however, the owner moved to Chicago to manage a restaurant. There, he collected some additional parts, including an original fairing. Unfortunately, he stored these rare bits at the restaurant, and a custodian, unaware of

This International
Norton was brought to
the United States by
a British expat in the
airline industry. Lee
Berghoff, discussed
in Chapter 7, took
detailed measurements
of this bike to make
a sculpture.

Here's the proud owner
of a primo survivor
bike shortly after
taking possession.
The seat has since
been changed to the
original solo setup.

Peter Martin

Colin Seeley built a winner in looks and performance, one that continues to excel at vintage races in reproduction form. This is the real deal.

what they were, got rid of them. That tragedy discouraged the owner, after which he put his lightweight race bike out of mind.

When Freaky Fred's owners decided to close their doors, the special Matchless was still there—and Hamel wanted it. Badly. It's a pure performance machine, designed without compromise, a mandate Hamel admires. He managed to connect with the Seeley owner's father, who met him at a local watering hole called Lendway's Lounge. There, in a familiar collector-world ritual, Hamel began laying down 100 dollar bills. When the owner's father was satisfied, he signed a bill of sale.

Loading the long-coveted Seeley into his 1963 Dodge van, Hamel had a feeling of conquest. It wouldn't last. The enclosed Mopar had some front-end problems of the sort only an ace mechanic will tolerate, because he insists on repairing his own vehicles but never has the time. Every so often, when pace and pavement condition were exactly wrong, the Dodge's front wheels launched into a death wobble, promising to throw van and occupants over the nearest embankment. Transporting the precious Seeley was a golden opportunity for the wobble gods, who patiently waited until Hamel turned onto a bridge spanning the Mississippi River.

On cue, the steering went into hula mode, lurching uncontrollably toward oncoming traffic, then the guardrail. Hamel crushed the brake pedal, hoping the Dodge had enough Volkswagen-style buoyancy to stay afloat while he crawled out the window if it came to it. Joyfully, the

A double drum brake operates by dual cables coming off the hand lever. The tachometer sits on its own perch protruding from the head tube.

Seeley's design has a modern feel even today. The engine bears no trace of the difficulties through which it put its former owner. Steve Hamel did a lot of work to get it right. In the end, he must be glad it had prior problems. Had it not, he wouldn't have encountered the bike at an area repair shop.

brake jolt broke the oscillation, and the van's road manners returned, impact free.

Hamel got his prize home and set it up in his shop, where it tipped over onto a caster-mounted work stool. The ride across town hadn't removed all the freaky. "When it happened, I couldn't believe it," Hamel says. "There's something eerie about a motorcycle lying on its side. It's unnatural."

The stool struck the aluminum gas tank with the inevitable result. Unfazed—angry and appalled, but unfazed—Hamel removed the tank, cut a section out of the bottom, and hammered out the dent. He then finished the work Freaky Fred's never got right. The engine

Hamel on his street Vincent, which is not all original, but it will soon be more so. He has recently found and purchased the frame members that match this Black Shadow engine. The shop in the background hosts about as much Vincent tuning as occurs anywhere in the world.

Longtime legend on a future survivor: Bonneville record-holder Marty Dickerson points Steve Hamel's well-tuned Vincent across the salt. Dickerson is 81 years old here, and the run he is about to make set a vintage record in 2007. While history has not yet made this Vincent a survivor, it will. Records bikes of old, unrestored from their heyday, are highly prized by collectors.

needed a cylinder, which the prior shop had replaced with a 350-unit set on a spacer for more stroke. Hamel found a Matchless enthusiast in Michigan selling a genuine 500-cylinder with broken fins. Hamel bought it, repaired the fins, and rebuilt the engine to proper spec. Now the Seeley-framed G50 is complete and looks superb.

Like the International's engine, and the miles the Italian bikes cry out for, the Seeley will get Hamel's full attention.

But not yet. First, there are the salt flats and the records Hamel plans to break there. His hero, Rollie Free, went a few decimal places more than 150 on alcohol in 1948. Hamel surpassed that mark, hitting about 152.4 in 2006. He needs about another 10 miles an hour to beat Free's best on alcohol, which was 160.7. Hamel would like to top that on gasoline, but it will take some engineering.

In the meantime, Hamel has befriended another Vincent legend, Marty Dickerson, who helped Free in 1950. Dickerson was an early Vincent promoter and dealer in California, and he set records of his own on the salt after Phil Vincent shipped him some hot rod parts.

In recent years, Dickerson has come to Bonneville as a spectator. Hamel met him there and threw out a crazy offer: "If I build you a bike, will you ride it?" Dickerson responded with an immediate and very definite "yes."

Time didn't allow Hamel to build a designated bike, so he offered his own Vincent for Dickerson's ride in 2007. On a marque synonymous with lakebed magic, Dickerson whipped Hamel's bike to an AMA vintage record 151.6 miles per hour—at age 81!

The following year, they planned to push it further, but Hamel had some problems with the bike that caused them to miss the Bub (Denis Manning's nickname) Speed Trials. Hamel went to the salt flats a bit later and made the speed trials for another sanctioning body, the USFRA (Utah Salt Flats Racing Association). He beat that organization's vintage record by 18 miles per hour. More records will fall as relentless hard work chips away at history's hurdles.

The boy who grew up with the wind in his face still chases the horizon and will keep chasing, looking for the best a motorcycle, a lakebed, and a legend can provide.

The best position
from which to enjoy a
Laverda SFC—that's
"C" for *competizione*.

CHAPTER 10

"That Flying Carrot"

Tim Parker's 1975 Laverda SFC 750

IN THE EARLY 1970S, the United Kingdom's Laverda importer faced an ambitious task: pitching Italian motorcycles to a nation steeped in its own bikes' history and now embracing fare from Japan. Amid Union Jacks and Rising Suns, what could draw buyers to the red, white, and green? The same things as always, of course: sexy lines and sophistication. Laverda's man in England, Roger Slater, had his Italian brothers' brochure-printer mixing love potion with the ink. One pamphlet went to Tim Parker, sparking a lifelong devotion to these beautiful, brutish bombshells on wheels.

Like a golf slice or a defensive tackle, love hits hardest when you're not looking. Parker wasn't after a particular make, just a big-twin road bike to pilot around and have some fun on. He wrote every manufacturer of big twins asking for literature. Only Slater responded—with his Mediterranean bike porn, the Laverda line.

Before then, motorcycles had not owned Parker's soul.

He got his first ride as a teenager. Unannounced, his father brought home an 80cc Suzuki for him and a Suzuki 50 for his brother. When Parker broke third gear on a trip to Scotland, he sent the Suzuki back to England on a British Road Services truck—which took all his money—then hitchhiked home. He bought the part he needed from the local Suzuki supplier, fixed the 80, and offered it to a big London bike dealer, who snapped it up.

After a high-maintenance fling with a Triumph TR3 roadster, on which he learned his mechanics, Parker got another bike through an acquaintance at work. A woman in typesetting at Haynes Publishing (Parker's employer) had a Velocette that needed to go. It was her

A fairing can make or break a motorcycle's lines, and this is part of why they get separated from many bikes as the years pass. Generally, factory designs look best. This one is spot on.

Heavier than its fastest peers, the flying carrot does quite well at speed. Tim Parker has softened the suspension, which improved racetrack handling. Though tweaked for speed, the 2-into-1 exhaust is a factory piece.

husband's in truth, but her wanting it gone was the operative detail. The bike went to Parker, in boxes, for £10.

A new staffer at Haynes had written a history of the marque that included a Velocette Scrambler, a more inspiring model than the 350cc MAC just cleared from the typesetter's home. Parker built up the Velo in that form, scrapping the original mill and hiring old-school

The windscreen fitted in 1975 got pitted and crazed to oblivion from track use and wear. This is a proper Laverda screen fitted in the 1980s when Parker used the bike on U.S. tracks.

Velocette engineer, Ralph Seymour, to build him a proper 500cc engine. The resulting scrambler knockoff looked great, yet it was hard to start and harder to ride.

Since his Suzuki 50 days, Parker's brother, John, had matured to more serious machines, including Norton's Commando. He told Parker to stop messing around with the Velocette and buy a proper road bike. It was that advice that prompted his inquiries to each motorcycle manufacturer. Slater's brochure was postage well spent. Parker went to the dealership, sat on the bikes, and drank in their glorious curves and tech. He left with a brand new SF2 750.

"I rode that bike to Monte Carlo through the Alps with two guys on R90S BMWs," Parker recalls—one of whom was Murray Walker, who would go on to become a well known Formula 1 announcer in Britain. "My SF2 couldn't keep up with them on the freeways, but in the mountains it would leave them. You could grind the exhaust system's cross-pipe in the turns when you were really knocking on."

The Japanese bikes were pouring into the market and the magazines, and for a time Parker gave them a try. He sold the SF2 and bought a Honda 550 Sport because of an article he'd seen in *Cycle World*, featuring one all tricked out with performance parts. Parker built his just like the magazine bike with lots of pieces imported from the United States. The rodded Honda was a looker but lacked the depth for a long-term relationship. "It was fast but no fun," Parker says.

Many speedometer needles, particularly those on collector-kept bikes, never cross the numbers on the big end of the dial. This is not a crime Parker has committed. Bike and rider have done the same dance, flat out.

He gave Japan another try, swapping the 550 for a new Suzuki GS 750, its first four-cylinder. It didn't thrill him like the Laverda had, so he traded that for a 750 SF3.

Could be these were just fickle times for Parker because that bike, too, failed to raise his pulse like his first Slater import, the SF2. "It just didn't go like the first one." But he wasn't leaving Laverda this time. Parker was in publishing and Slater was interested in putting together a Laverda book, so they struck a deal. Parker would bang out the text, and Slater would pay him with a fresh steed from his Welsh Border stables, a 1200 triple.

When Parker delivered the book in 1978, he gave Slater an address for the bike. It wasn't his own. He was moving up the food chain to an SFC, Laverda's thinly veiled race bike sold for the street for maximum market potential. The SF Competizione was a rare bike, with less than 550 produced. Incredibly, Parker found a patent agent who'd hoarded three of them. The book-trade 1200 went to this agent, new in the crate, and Parker took home the bright orange 1975 Laverda you see here. The tank is oversized because the Competizione was designed for 24-hour racing.

"The SFC is a fantastic bike," Parker beams. "It's harsh, noisy, heavy—very strong, very reliable, and fast as hell in a 1970s context." Even his criticism hints at praise. "I rode it on the street in London. Terrible. You need to be a wrestler to pull the clutch lever, . . . but when

The modified side cover houses the electronic ignition, another factory modification for more civilized behavior. The frame shows off grease, to its owner's chagrin, but it's a track runner not a trailer queen. Some character marks are to be expected.

you leaned over, lying on that tank . . ." Fond memories of blurred scenery returned.

"I went to Donington Park racetrack for a test day on the SFC," Parker says. "I lived about 160 miles from Donington and the first 60 or 70 miles were countryside. You just blat through it. The SFC could sit on the freeway at 90 or 100." That's about the speed he was going when he passed a busload of London journalists headed to the track. When they parked, one of them marched up to Parker: "You were very irresponsible passing the bus like that at 100 miles an hour," he shot. The man's colleagues looked at their peer in surprise. There was no mistaking how they viewed the matter: They'd have traded lurching about on a bus seat for slicing the wind on the faired 750 without stopping either vehicle. Perhaps it was jealousy that got their bus mate bent out of shape.

Parker raced the bike several times; it had been competed since new. At one event, fast racer-journalist Ray Knight approached him and his Laverda at trackside. "Be very careful on that flying carrot," Knight quipped. Parker was, then and each time out. Carving up a race course with peers is fast fun, but he had no aspirations of becoming a pro. A little competitive amateur racing was an ample adrenaline fix, one more likely to preserve the Laverda and its rider.

When Parker moved to the States to join Motorbooks International Publishing a few years later, he contacted the local classic motorcycle and racing clubs. He joined the Central Roadracing Association, an amateur racing club, for an event at the expansive Brainerd International Raceway in Minnesota. By now, his SFC had logged many hard-pushed miles. Asking it again to put the competition behind, Parker could feel that his low-production Laverda was wearing out. Though built for strength, the engine was no longer making impressive power. It felt like an old bike.

He asked around for a good race tuner, and the name Steve Ferree kept coming up. Parker contacted him, and Ferree said he was interested in helping him develop the SFC. "I told him to make it powerful and make it reliable," Parker says. Ferree did, machining and mixing in American and Japanese parts, like cut-down Manley small-block Chevy exhaust valves with Yamaha guides and seals—real hot rod engineering. The single coil with two wires went in favor of two Boschs with one wire apiece. Stock Borrani wheels were pretty but not strong enough, so off they came, swapped for Akront rims spoked in stainless steel by California wheel builder, Buchanan.

Out back, the Laverda rear hub is a magnesium alloy that isn't quite up to racing torque loads. The spokes elongate the holes in the flange. Parker searched across manufacturers for a disk-brake rear hub with the same axle diameter. Only the Suzuki GS 750 worked. California's Sandy Kosman did a one-off custom disk and disk mounting, which Ferree fitted along with a stock caliper and stock axle. For the right piston size, Grimeca master cylinder took over for the stock Brembo.

With the engine running right and the bike stopping well, the tuner had a final tweak for Parker's SFC: "The most important change we need to make," Ferree said, "is to soften the suspension." If race tune and harsh ride seem conjoined, in the SFC's case the unforgiving shocks were costing the bike responsiveness. The needed swaps proved to be reworked Kawasaki springs up front and Ohlins gas shocks off a Suzuki at the rear. "Preloaded right," Parker says, "the ride is very compliant and relatively soft."

These changes got the competition Laverda out of the blocks, across the straights, and through the turns faster than it had ever moved before. In amateur races, Parker usually ran near the front, finishing in

Keep in mind that those clicks are kilometers. This mini-sport bike was almost new when Parker got it, and he put on about 5,000 enjoyable miles.

A 1984 LB 125 Sport looks to be the opposite end of the Laverda performance spectrum, yet it's comfortable, reliable, and capable of 80 miles per hour. In its day, the little Laverda was every teenage Italian male's dream.

the lead group among Ducatis and other Laverdas and ahead of the Commandos and less advanced fare fighting at the back of the pack.

The Laverda's big race tune for U.S. soil was more than 20 years ago. Today, the Slater-sold, patent-agent-traded, Ferree-tuned Laverda

This bike looks totally restored, yet everything but the tires is what the factory fitted. It's a pretty nice looking machine for a 125 and an uncommon find in the United States.

750 SF Competizione is just as it was after its amateur racing came to an end. The paint and all parts not refreshed in the course of its track life are what the factory applied in 1975. This bike has appeared in numerous books and articles and for a number of years sat at the front of the Motorbooks offices in Saint Paul, Minnesota, lending that extra bit of authenticity to the car and motorcycle publisher.

While the SFC has left the biggest tire print on Parker's soul, he has several other Laverdas picked up in the decades since the marque first caught his eye. His LB 125 Sport might be the only one of its kind in the United States. Parker bought it in 1984 in London. An Australian was the prior owner, though only by accident. The Aussie had flown to Italy to buy a Moto Guzzi, but through bad luck or poor judgment—or both—his money got stolen. He only had enough left for the little Laverda, which he bought in Florence, rode to London, and then sold to fly home.

The dealer who took it in knew Parker and his fixation on Laverda. He rang and said, "You won't believe. I've got an LB 125 for sale." Parker hung up the phone, drove directly to the dealership, and bought it. He rode it around England a bit, then brought it to the United States. It's covered only about 7,000 kilometers and still wears its English license plate from 1984. The little two-stroke is extremely original and unrestored. The tires are about the only parts not fitted by the factory.

Parker has also accumulated a rare mid-1960s 125cc Sport, a 100 from the 1950s, and a 50cc mini-scooter with lines more or less like a Vespa. He has some more modern bikes from other manufacturers, though they'd probably be Laverdas, too, if the company was still in business.

It's been more than 30 years since he acted on his older brother's suggestion to "get a proper road bike." With his purchases, collection, books, and enthusiasm, Parker has done about as much as anyone to further the Laverda name. Although the motorcycles have come and gone, Parker remains friends with the maker's winning U.K. agent, Roger Slater.

There were a lot of motorcycle dealers in the U.K. back in the early 1970s. Wonder what might have happened on the racetracks and the bookshelves if any them had been serious enough about their product to send an eager prospective customer a little brochure. No matter. For Tim Parker, the one that responded is the only one that counts. When the Italians win your heart, the competition disappears.

Read all the specs and reviews you want, the genuine enjoyment captured here is as good an endorsement of the bike as you'll find. Outside temperature for this photo was about 15 degrees Fahrenheit.

Many manufacturers in the United States combined a motor and a bicycle. Succeed or fail, they're all winners now.

YANKEE
IRON

Long handlebars often characterize early "street" bikes, *street* being a euphemism in those days. Old-time riders say they would sometimes hold the grips at the ends where they could flex and absorb vibration.

CHAPTER 11

The Deacon's Wards

Deke Diegal's 1912 Yale and 1920 Merkel

"Deke" Diegal got his nickname in school from kids he used to babysit for a little pocket money. His wards found him strict but fair, for which they dubbed him "the Deacon." Looking after things, improving their lot in life when he can, suits Deke to this day. Many bikes have come into his hands since he began collecting in the 1980s. He has restored those that were too rusty or incomplete to stand on their own, but good luck and a watchful eye have brought several interesting unrestored machines his way, including a 1912 Yale twin, 1920 Merkel Motor Wheel, and a little 1967 Allstate Compact that looks almost new.

A Yale twin would be a heart-racing find today. Yet in the 1950s postwar boom, primitive machines from the early years of motorcycle manufacturing attracted little interest. Deke's Yale was a giveaway at an auction in 1956 or 1957. It was slated for sale, yet when it came across the block, there were no bidders—none, for any price. Charged with moving all of the merchandise offered for bid, the auctioneer got creative. He called up the next item, a '33 or '34 Ford, and announced that the winner of that vehicle would receive the motorcycle as well.

Having excited only crickets on its own merits, the '12 Yale was little more than a spare object to haul home for the Ford's winning bidder. He kept it, though, storing it indoors and protected. He told Deke that he had hoped to get it running someday, but the freebie antique two-wheeler never made it to first place on the Ford owner's to-do list. He had his cars, so an early motorcycle, with room for only one traveler, no weather protection, and inadequate power to run with modern traffic, just sat.

After storing it more than 25 years, the auction winner sold it to Deke, who was eager to see to its needs. Deke went through the bike's

Yale built a pretty V-twin, distinguished from competitors' engines by its parallel fins. Perhaps designers paid particular attention to this feature because the engine, overall, resembles the "Y" in the company logo.

On more recent motorcycles, we might look for both a kick start and electric starter. In the old days, the transition was from pedals to footpegs, the former being useful for help on hills, or when fuel ran out. This 1912 Yale Model 27 was rated at 7 horsepower.

mechanicals and had an engine expert get the seven-horse V-twin back in operating form. The bike now runs and is sturdy enough to carry the Deacon, who at 6 feet 8 inches is a more formidable rider than the average motorcyclist of 1912.

The Model 27 is well preserved, escaping the scrap heap—which so many bikes of the period didn't do when they had little following—and also ducking restoration, the route much of the remaining early cycles have gone since collectors did start taking an interest. The Consolidated Manufacturing Company, Yale's builder, made motorcycles for only three more years before switching to materiel production for the Great War. They never returned to bikes, making unrestored Yale twin owners a rarified club.

Another antique treasure to come Deke's way is a 1920 Merkel Motor Wheel, which likewise sat ignored for decades, though not for the same reason as the Yale. The Merkel was hanging from the rafters in a Midwest granary, affixed to a Napoleon bicycle. A friend of Deke's bought it and—tale of a thousand projects—hoped to get it running, but didn't. Deke talked him out of it a decade ago.

Investing himself in worthy projects, helping them reach their potential, is a Diegal specialty. When an ingenious antiquated motor-vehicle has evaded destruction against great odds and found its way, mute, to the present day, Deke loves to step in and restoke its huffing and chuffing voice. The Merkel-powered Napoleon posed a few challenges, however, including a stuck motor and a damaged front rim. The latter was as big a problem as the engine because the rims, while metal-spoked like a modern bicycle's, are made of wood and not readily repaired or replaced.

Deke enjoys working on his bikes, but he leaves machine work to pros. Fortunately, he found a shop in Oregon experienced not only with old motorcycle engines but with Merkel Motor Wheels themselves. Mike and Matthew Smith at Antique Motorcycle Works in Oregon had a bolt-on Merkel bike pusher of their own and knew the engine's specs and secrets. They're also creative machinists, which was important with Deke's Merkel. His engine's bronze connecting rod was worn out beyond sleeving, so they built it up and used it to cast a new one, which they then machined to proper size. A rocker arm

Apart from being ingenious, a motor wheel is a logical component in an antique motorcycle collection—a symbolic (and reversible!) "missing link" between bicycle and motorbike.

Deke Diegal's Merkel-driven bicycle derives some freebie historic feel, compliments of its name. Given its age, the tin badge is in extraordinary condition.

needed welding and one of the two valves had bent and was replaced. In addition, the Smiths reground the crank and replaced the rings and seals—standard rebuild stuff.

Although typical fare on the inside, this engine work differed from that of a restored bike in one critical respect: Deke instructed them to leave the Merkel's patina intact. He wanted them to make the engine run properly but not to polish away the grime or surface imperfections. The Smiths are known for such survivor-quality work, which is part of why Deke chose them. They got the bolt-on one-cylinder in good running condition and shipped the whole bike back to Deke.

Despite being considerably bigger than the boys and teenagers who were the Motor Wheel's primary market, Deke would probably take this clever two-wheeler for a spin, too, were it not for that damaged front wheel. Fortunately, he's managed to find another wood rim, virtually identical to the Napoleon's but in solid shape, that he's ready to swap in—returning the machine's roadworthiness while preserving its patina. He had a veteran repairman experienced with antique rims

Simple though it is, an original throttle is one of the more difficult components to find. Diegal has had several offers for this part alone. Those offers were refused, of course.

The Merkel motor needed some repairs when Diegal got it, but he was fortunate to find a shop familiar with them. They performed an age-sensitive rebuild, leaving surface tarnish and patina intact.

lined up to swap them. Sadly, like the vehicles themselves, these old craftsmen are a vanishing breed and the man passed away before he could do the job. You can bet Deke will find another skillful soul to give this project the attention it deserves.

Another noteworthy feature of Deke's motor wheel is the bike it's attached to. The Merkel Motor Wheel was purchased by Hendee Manufacturing Company in 1918 and most of them are believed to have been fitted to Indian bicycles. Someone may have purchased Deke's motor separately, or perhaps the owner of the original machine wrecked the bicycle or decided that propelling it under his own power was more fun and sold off the driven wheel. It's easy enough to swap. The whole drive unit goes on and off as easily as the bike's own hubs. Just unbolt the stock axle nuts, remove the factory wheel, and slide the motor wheel into place. Affix the rather honking shift lever—did George Hurst have an ancestor at work in this period?—and a throttle lever, and off you go.

Antique American bikes hold a special fascination for Deke, though he isn't one to take sides in the Indian vs. Harley-Davidson rivalry. Either brand is fine, and he has alluring examples of both in his collection, including two Silent Gray Fellows that he restored. They were too battered by the elements to leave as is, but there was something there worth saving. "When I see things that need help—all rusty, paint gone—I feel sorry for them," he says. "I think, 'I'll bring this thing back to life.'"

Deke started collecting old motorcycles in the 1980s, which in his case involved buying basket cases and putting them together. "I bought quite a few," he says. "I didn't get at restoring them right away, but I worked on them here and there. I'd find parts and assemble it."

Even in the 1990s, an antique bike could still find its way to the scrap pile—which with bikes, old cars, and tractors, is a literal term. An age-old path for such machinery is to be uncovered on rural property—found by family members or youngsters out looking to make a couple of bucks—and cut up or loaded up and taken to a scrap yard. Such recycled steel is an important component of modern manufacturing. Maybe there's a little Yale or Merkel in your Super Glide.

One of Deke's shiny Silent Grey Fellows came from a scrap iron pile. Some kids cleaning out an old resort in Bemidji, Minnesota,

Deke Diegal collection

Restored and unrestored bikes are welcome in Diegal's garage. Anything he buys that's original but too far gone, he'll bring back to former glory. This stunning 1948 Indian Chief has been redone to perfection.

found it lying against a fence. It was caked in rust—patina had come and gone long before—and they hauled it to the place where old metal goes, no doubt with other objects of less historic significance. Deke got wind of it, drove out to the scrap yard, and paid at least its value in raw steel. He then put in the time to track down missing pieces and replace what was damaged or decayed beyond rescue. Looking at that rejuvenated bike next to the Yale offers a striking reminder of the difference between restoration and preservation. The old Harley went from new . . . to used . . . to weathered . . . to virtually unrecognizable in its deterioration—and then back to its new appearance, again. The Yale, a few years older, is frozen in a state of patina the restored bike passed through and left behind. Such is the special nature of the survivor, which wears its age like a living creature.

Sometimes a bike Deke buys doesn't need much saving—just a good home. That was the case with his Allstate Compact scooter, which he bought at an auction because it was in superb original condition. "It's so nice—and original paint—just like it came from the showroom," Deke says. "There's a couple chips on the floorboards; that's about it." For a humble little scootabout sold by Sears—for whom

The Puch-built Allstate Compact was sold by Sears. Apart from minor chips on the floorboards, this one is immaculate and unrestored.

Austria's Puch built them—the Compact has a fair amount of style. The rounded gas tank evokes a motorcycle's, and the two-tone paint scheme has retro charm. It has been properly stored and cared for as the finish is unfaded on both the bike and seat. Likewise, the single gauge, a speedometer, is in perfect condition, showing only 1,091 miles on its odometer. Funny that the three unrestored vehicles in his collection are among the smallest, apart from a restored Doodlebug. "Everybody's gotta have a Doodlebug," Deke says.

Since the 1980s, the Deacon has collected about a dozen motorcycles, a machine he's admired since childhood. "When I was a kid,

When the mileage is this low, collectors debate whether using the vehicle at all is worth it. Owners can do whatever brings them the most pleasure, though collector value will stay highest at nominal miles.

The fuel tank is a touchstone for condition. Faded, dented, and rusty, and we downgrade our impressions. Careful storage has kept the Compact's most visible feature free of dents, scratches, and fading. Even the logo looks identical to new.

old Harleys and Indians were running around," he recalls. "Back then money was pretty scarce in our family." Deke started sweeping floors and eventually got a job at an auto upholstery shop, which needed a guy to take seats out of cars. His long reach facilitated that work, but Deke's also good with hands and pretty soon he was handling upholstery work too. Eventually, he started his own business.

Custom upholstery is popular on the car circuit, and Deke's done some of that work. Mostly, though, he likes to do with cars as he does with his bikes: keeping the original look. He used to collect cars, too, and once had a Ranchero, El Camino, '55 Buick Special convertible, '56 Ford hardtop, '57 Ford convertible, '64 Chevy SS convertible, '64 Lincoln convertible, '29 Model A, and a '66 Caddy limo that he did modify a bit, installing a TV. "I used to let the neighbor kids take that car to their proms," he says. His rules with the limo were strict—but fair. He's since sold off all the cars except the Buick, which he's got room for at home.

It's just as well the car collection is gone because when the weather is warm, Deke mostly rides his motorcycles. For long trips, he's got an '07 Harley that he put 11,500 miles on last year. Not bad in a northern clime whipped by snowstorms half the time.

Deke's got one more hobby that combines motorcycles and his love for old-time machinery. Toward the end of each summer, he joins a small group of friends in Wyoming, rekindling the spirit of the West. He rides the Harley down and they shoot single-action .45 pistols "like the old cowboy days," Deke says.

"I'm not good at it," he laughs, "but I have fun."

He's got the name for it too. When you ride an iron horse into a Wyoming town to shoot six guns with friends, you couldn't pick a better nickname than the Deacon. His character's a good fit too. As he's proven with cars and motorcycles for much of his life, when it's time to restore order, or get the job done, Deke's a good man to call.

One bike and one best gal. What John Eiden loves, he keeps.

CHAPTER 12

One'll Do

John Eiden's 1944 Harley-Davidson WLA

THERE'S A DIFFERENCE between American generations that goes beyond parents thinking their children like bad music. Since the last world war, the United States has fallen into a disposable lifestyle. The things we've thrown out, outgrown, and lost interest in heap landfills high and litter the landscape. That's not how John Eiden was raised, and it isn't how he lives. If a good thing works, he keeps it. If it breaks, he fixes it. In his many years enjoying and serving his country, he has owned one motorcycle—the Harley-Davidson WLA he bought new in 1946.

Eiden served in World War II as an electronics technician, training servicemen to repair radar and communications equipment. After Germany surrendered, he worked with military intelligence in China. There, he observed Harley-Davidsons on convoy duty, their riders guiding truck movements through tricky terrain. Watching bikers leap a washout, the rear wheel arcing through the air to slam down and keep right on going, left an impression on Eiden. These were sturdy machines—and they looked fun!

The U.S. military purchased a lot of Harleys for the war. When it ended, there were a few left over. Veterans who were honorably discharged could pick one up, new in the crate. Eiden bought his from the Springfield, Illinois, depot for $370 and had it freighted to the Twin Cities. He assembled it in his uncle's garage. It was a military-spec bike—the A in WLA means "Army"—with blacked-out lights, armor plate on the bottom, and a rifle scabbard. Eiden "civilianized" it, removing the military components for a peacetime look.

The WLAs worked hard in the service, but that wasn't his plan for this bike. "I just chased around," he says. He rode through a winter or

Olive drab green wasn't cutting it with the ladies, so Eiden sprayed his WLA blue, keeping the O.D. as basecoat. The color was an immediate hit, and it's held up more than 60 years.

two with a sidecar to stay upright in Minnesota snow, then switched to cars for daily transportation. He bought a '36 Ford in 1948 and had several Renaults beginning in the 1960s: a Dauphine, R 12, and Le Car. He'd buy them cheap and fix them himself.

Initially, Eiden kept the Harley olive drab, "but I had to paint it," he says, "because it wouldn't attract any girls." He bought an air compressor and a spray gun, which he still has, and practiced on a 55-gallon drum. "When the drum looked pretty good, I switched over to blue paint and sprayed my tank and fenders." The original Army paint is still there, underneath. "That OD green was the best primer

Harley made 'em good for the war effort. This is the original fender. The three bolts (one missing) along the side of the fender held a chrome trim piece in the bike's early days. Compare this with the black-and-white photo.

paint you ever saw," he maintains. Considering the bike still wears the bright blue coat he sprayed in 1947, he must be right.

The blue proved a good choice, acceptable to the fairer sex. He courted his wife, Annette, on the Harley and even got engaged on it in 1950, though not the way he intended. Annette was holding onto him on the back of the bike while Eiden had the ring in his shirt pocket. She found it and put it on her finger. "Isn't that pretty?" she called into the wind.

"I was looking for a more auspicious moment," Eiden laughs. They didn't even stop the bike.

In answer to an obvious question—why just the one?—Eiden explains, "I'm not a motorcycle hobbyist." Yet modesty marks the man and his generation. He's ridden the war-surplus Harley more than

Wider windscreen blocks more frigid air in wintertime, protecting the rider's hands.

100,000 miles and done all the work himself. Apart from perishable items, plus a reverse gear he fitted for sidecar use, the engine is about the only thing that isn't original. It's a proper WLA engine, war-surplus like his bike. He got it about 1958, when a local wrecking yard was being displaced by riverfront development. As they started selling things off, the yard discovered a half-dozen military surplus Harley engines that the owner hadn't even realized were there. Eiden got word of them and decided a spare was a pretty good idea. He rushed over and got the last one, still in its military shipping crate, for $75.

Fortunately, he still has the original engine too, which he pulled because it was starting to smoke. It's in a box in the garage, waiting for a rebuild from its industrious owner. Eiden's done the job before with help from his brother, a machinist. His brother gives him the measurements, and Eiden takes it from there.

Eiden's youth is a lot different from what today's kids know. He grew up on a farm in Holdingford, Minnesota, 1 of 13 children. They had no running water or electricity and kept in touch with the world through his parents' battery-operated radio. Eiden was intrigued by radios. He took them apart, figured out how they worked, and began fixing them.

"I'd go to farmers' stone piles and get their old radios and all the batteries I could find," he says. "I'd bring them back to my radio shack"—a shed, not the corporation—"and make one I could listen to myself."

He also made some money helping farmers get their new radio sets going. He'd climb a tree, put up a big antenna, then drive a ground post, hook up the battery, and help the farmer tune in the first station. He received 50 cents to a dollar for helping farm families hear what he enjoyed: news and entertainment from around the world. Radios were a welcome luxury for a family that bathed in a washtub with rainwater heated on the kitchen stove. That was the drill for the Eiden clan, all 15 of them. The youngest got the bath water first, and they'd continue through the whole family to his father, always last.

The sidecar is also a winter add-on, giving the WLA a three-point stance when snow falls.

Besides the radio, the only other convenience they had in Eiden's childhood was a Briggs and Stratton–powered washing machine. "Dad's prestige went up a couple notches when he brought that home," Eiden recalls. "We had a hand-powered one before that." If you're wondering about internal combustion appliances for indoor use, the

John Eiden modified the transmission, adding a reverse gear for sidecar use along with an appropriate shifter gate.

family would run the exhaust pipe out the window and put blankets on either side. As was his nature, Eiden tinkered with the new washer too. "I took apart and reworked the magneto," he says, "and bumped it up. It was kind of weak."

He was "one of those technical nerds," he admits, skills that took him to Univac after the war. Company headquarters were on the East Coast, but they had production facilities in various places, including Saint Paul, Minnesota. Eiden called on customers around the country, servicing what were then advanced computers. The Great Northern Railroad had one it used to keep track of its boxcars. "It was all vacuum tubes," Eiden remembers. "You'd walk inside to repair it."

The Harley-rider electronics expert even got to work with NASA. "Apollo 13 had made them jumpy," he says. "For Apollo 15 they had a telemetry system that was old for its time. I knew the old equipment." So Univac sent him to Houston to help get our astronauts to the moon and back without any movie-grade drama.

Eiden's bike was built in 1944 and delivered, per the identification plate shown previously, on April 24, 1945.

While his electronics job was challenging and interesting, it was still work. It's the war-era Harley that was—and is—his true ticket to fun. From 1946 to 1952, Eiden rode with the Gypsy Motorcycle Club, one of many groups started in major cities at the behest of the Harley-Davidson factory. Clubs gave motorcycles publicity and their riders more ways to socialize and enjoy the road, with picnics and group rides, plus appearances and assistance at local events. Eiden and the Gypsies escorted the Minneapolis Aquatennial Parade, a well known Twin Cities celebration, for several years. The parade coordinator joined them on a motorcycle.

If most of this riding was calmer than the harsh, tense treks through a war-torn landscape, bikers still had a hunger to test themselves and their motorcycles off-road. Every fall, the Gypsies took their street bikes on a "cross-country" run, one of Eiden's favorite outings. He'd join his club mates on his WLA, charging through cornfields, gravel pits, stone piles, and dry river bottoms. It was a timed event, clocked by women who were club members or friends.

There were several women who rode with the Gypsies. One had an Ariel Square Four, and another owned a '46 61-cubic inch Harley-Davidson Knucklehead. "She was such a little gal—it was too big," Eiden remembers. "When she kick-started it once, she didn't retard the spark. It kicked back and she got thrown up on top of the windshield." She had spirit, which the men in the club appreciated—especially

The engine in the WLA is not the original, though it is a proper war surplus Harley engine purchased from a wrecking yard. This is the original engine, which Eiden will keep with the bike. He may rebuild it.

the one who married her. Eiden's still in touch with a few fellow club members from those days.

Another pastime booming in the 1950s and 1960s—and helping to sell motorcycles—was racing. Eiden was good friends with some area racers, including Harley dealer Johnny Ekberg. Ekberg ran Indians before that company went broke, then switched to Harleys. Eiden remembers Ekberg complaining after one race, "I wish I had my Indian." The Harley WR he ran would go around turns but wasn't good in the straight-aways, where the Indians would pull away.

Eiden watched a lot of racing at state and county fairgrounds. Once, on the way to the TT races at White Bear Lake, Minnesota, he got a flat tire on his WLA. Fortunately, the war-surplus repair kit was still in the saddlebags. He took off the tire, patched the tube, and used the military-issue hand pump to get the front tire up to 15 psi. He felt it had all gone well and was happy to be back on his way to the races, until he realized everyone was now coming home from them in the oncoming lanes.

Though more practical than competitive, Eiden decided to try some racing himself. Why not? He was an experienced rider, and he kept his Harley in good tune. The amateur level was Class C, which required riders to compete on the bike they rode to and from the track. Eiden stripped it down, removing parts such as the headlight and front fender to cut weight. Start position was determined by individual

We shot these photos on a very cold day. I worried about keeping Eiden outside for long, until I remembered he's twice as tough as we are.

Here's the summer windscreen. Annette Eiden doesn't ride now, but she still appreciates the other constant in John's life.

Rick Schunk

time trials. Running alone, Eiden carved up the half-mile track in the second-fastest time.

Once in the race, though, things didn't unfold as he expected. "I thought the other guys were so rude," he laughs. "They cut me off, and I came in last. You had to be darned aggressive, and that's not my personality." He adds, "I think they had some experience."

Another thing he tried was the long, solitary journey emblematic of the biker lifestyle in a big, open country. He was courting Annette at the time and decided to take a solo trip on the Harley before marriage and children became the center of his world. "I said, 'I'm going to

Denver, and I'll be back in one-and-a-half weeks.' I got to Yankton, South Dakota, and said to myself, 'Why the heck am I doing this?' I turned around and went home." Being with Annette was where he really wanted to be. She was his riding partner in the early years, giving it up when she got pregnant with their first child.

Just when Eiden was going to retire, Annette met the editor of the Antique Motorcycle Club's newsletter at the bank. They got to talking about old motorcycles and she said her husband had one. He told her to have him join the club. Eiden did, and he's been enjoying the stories, rides, and company ever since.

He takes his Harley to Sturgis every year (by trailer), where it's always a hit. "I get the thumbs up," he says. "When I parked it in front of the hotel in Deadwood, a man came up to me. 'Were you in World War II?' he asked. 'Yeah.' He said, 'Let me shake your hand. Thank you very much.'"

Sixty-three years since he built it in his uncle's garage, the military Harley serves Eiden well and year-round. He doesn't hesitate to put his cross-country skis in the sidecar and ride out to a park to enjoy some snow and freezing temperatures.

"I keep having fun," he says, and he's never needed any other motorcycle to do it.

When a man came into the shop to ask Del Hofer if he worked on old motorcycles, he hardly expected to see something like this.

CHAPTER 13

Harley Man for Life

Del Hofer's Motor Company Marvels

THERE'S A SIMPLE TEST for the motorcycle gene. Ease your weight into the saddle, gaze across the bars at an open stretch of road, crank on some throttle, and let that whirring mill launch you into the future— and you'll know. If the rush that flashes through you overcomes any sense of fear, you've got it. Harnessing that thrill, refining those skills, will make your life feel more complete.

Del Hofer took the bars of his older brother's bike at age 14. Test came back positive.

For the next two years, Del hunted for a ride of his own. When he found "the one," it set all those first-bike dreams in motion. The bike was a '47 Harley-Davidson Knucklehead, price $250. That was a lot of money for a 16-year-old in 1950, but Del was motivated. He got a job delivering telegrams for Western Union for 28 bucks a week. He managed to set aside 25 of that from each paycheck.

As soon as he had the magic sum, Del closed the deal. Only hitch was, he hadn't let his mother in on his glorious plan. She saw the unfamiliar motorcycle outside the house and asked whose it was. When Del said it was his, she told him she was going to return it. Del replied, "You may as well keep the money then, because I won't be here when you get home."

Del's mother went into the house, upset. Many whims seize youthful minds, making it hard for parents to know which ones they're serious about. When she came back out, she didn't have a fresh argument, however; she had a camera. If her younger son was determined to own a motorcycle, she felt she should capture the moment. Neither of them knew at the time just how much this machine would come to define his future.

The paint has held up remarkably well, particularly on the tank, thanks in large part to the original owner's long use of the 1919 Harley throughout his life.

For five years, Del rode his proud purchase, then sold it when he enlisted in the Air Force. Another five years passed, serving his country, before Del returned to civilian life in need of a career. As he looked into his heart for a passion he could devote himself to, one thing stood out: the motorcycle he worked so hard to acquire as a boy. The machine that had inspired him years before, still did. Del borrowed $2,500 and started a Harley-Davidson dealership in 1961. Ten years later, he took over the Motor Company's store in Fargo, North Dakota.

Ski attachments were not fitted by the original owners, but they are a period aftermarket accessory. Hofer got them with some other vintage parts, and they bolted up easily to the Model J.

What began with a black '47 Knucklehead parked outside his childhood home has grown into 50 years of riding, and then selling, bikes from his favorite builder. In a half-century of motorcycling, Del has acquired many friends, stories, and a number of exceptional unrestored bikes. When a special Harley-Davidson comes along, Hofer the Harley dealer is no less determined to bring it home than the industrious telegram courier he saw in the mirror at 16.

One of Del's most spectacular finds stands on display in the dealership he's run for 48 years. It has been in the Fargo area since new. That bike came his way from a man who entered the store one day to ask if Del got old motorcycles running. Del said he did, so the man gave him an address and asked him to come and pick one up. When Del arrived, the man led him into his garage and pulled an old bed sheet off the bike. It was a 1919 Model J. The man said it had belonged to his father, who rode it regularly during his life. He passed it on to this man, who seldom took it out. Although more than 60 years old at the time, the bike was still in solid original condition.

Over the years, Del got to know the man, whose name was Henry. He was an engineer who had helped to build the Oahe Dam in Pierre,

The original mileage sits at under 16,000.

A factory-built sidecar bike in original condition. The first owner bought it so that his wife could join him in motorcycle travels.

South Dakota, in the 1950s. Del had worked for the railroad during this period supplying materials for the dam, an important project for the region. They had many conversations about this vast construction effort and the skills and manpower required to make it happen. Eventually, Henry reached a point where he had no further use for the '19 Harley. He told Del he could have it, an arrangement Henry's son finalized when the engineer passed away.

The bike is not exactly as it was when Henry and his father had it. Today, it wears a peculiar pair of attachments that Del got with some motorcycle parts he bought out of Idaho in the mid-1990s. The purchase included a sidecar, and when Del unpacked it, he found a pair of skis inside designed to mount on bikes like the Model J. This curious accessory was built for riders in snowy regions, allowing them to put their feet down when traction got dicey. Instead of stepping on the ground, the rider stepped onto the spring-loaded skis, which dropped to the snow and slid, allowing the rider to take the bike's weight and keep it from toppling, just as one can do at a standstill.

A sidecar features in another of Del's bikes, acquired from its original owners. Back when Del's store was the only Harley dealership in the state, enthusiasts would drop by from towns near and far. One regular visitor was a mechanic from Valley City, North Dakota, who would come with his wife. She had a disability, so he had ordered his bike with a factory-matched sidecar, in which she could join him on rides. The '65 FLH was in excellent original condition. Del told him if he ever wanted to sell or trade the combo, he was interested. In 1993, he told Del he was ready. His wife was no longer riding, so he traded the sidecar rig to Del for a brand new full dresser.

In addition to bringing their own rare machines to his attention, Del's customers sometimes mention bikes other people own that might interest him. One Saturday in 1984, the Harley seller was restoring a 1950 Panhead he owned. (This was before the Internet made pictures and details of just about everything as close as the nearest computer.) Del mentioned to a customer that he didn't remember what the front headlight necklace looked like. His customer said, "Why don't you ask Sid Sandie in Moorhead [Minnesota]. He has one." Del called and explained his situation. His fellow '50 Panhead owner said, "Sure, come over and look at it."

What Del saw in Moorhead answered his headlight question. It also surprised him. This 34-year-old bike was one of the most original Harley-Davidsons of its era that he had seen. The owner had been

The marbled handgrip is a period component with a lot of style.

What began as an information trip to check out an original 1950 Panhead quickly became an offer to buy it when Hofer learned the owner was no longer riding it. In all his years as a Harley rider and dealer, Hofer has seen no classic bike more original than this one.

an aviator in World War II, enjoying some of the same freedom on a motorcycle after the war. He had ridden the bike for many years and kept it well maintained, yet he was done with riding now. Del asked him what he was planning to do with it, and Sid said he wasn't sure. He had no children and no one in mind to will it to when he died. Del said that in that case, it would probably go in an estate sale and might get cut up for a chopper.

Sid replied, "No way in hell would that happen." Del shared his wish that the bike would stay original, but after Sid checked out, he wouldn't have any say in what happened to it. The former aviator looked at his new friend and asked what Del would do. "If you sell it to me," Del said, "I'll never let it be chopped, and I'll let people look at it as long as I live." He offered Sid market value for the bike, and the veteran said he would think about it.

Monday morning the phone rang. It was Sid. He asked when Del was coming to pick up his motorcycle. "Right away," came the

reply. When Del handed over the check, Sid said, "You can just as well take this along with you. I use it for weight in the trunk of my car in the winter, and it's of no use to me." With that, he uncovered a 1928 Excelsior Super X motor. He also threw in lowers and a winter shield for the '50 FL, along with a complete 1947 Jawa motorcycle.

With their mutual interests in bikes and stories, Del and Sid stayed in touch. Del appreciated Sid's adventures as an aviator fighting the German war machine for the fate of the free world. And both men enjoyed talking about motorcycling. In one of their discussions, Sid mentioned a friend he used to ride with who also had a '50 Panhead, though it was fitted with a '47 Knucklehead motor. These were special numbers to Del, who purchased his '47 Knucklehead in 1950. He asked the man's name and gave him a call.

Ernie Wicklund was as much a gentleman as Sid and happy to speak to another Harley enthusiast. He told Del he still had the FL and that they could go have a look at it. When they met, Ernie drove out to

This vintage Harley clock is a nice collectible. When it says Harley-Davidson, people want it. He gets offers on these items, just as with the motorcycles that are actually for sale.

When Japanese bikes started flooding showrooms cheap, Harley's little Italian-sourced Leggero lost buyers. Rather than lose money on it, Hofer pushed it into his warehouse.

a farm he used to own. The machine shed was still standing and when they entered it, there was his old Pan-knuckle-head. They cut a deal for the bike, after which Del asked if he could respond to a nature call behind the barn. What he found back there was more than a secluded spot for a leak. There was a 1937 Buick four-door sedan on blocks. It was Ernie's, and he had put it on blocks to keep the chassis from sitting on the ground and rotting. He had also put diesel fuel in the engine to prevent it from seizing up. Del bought the car, too, and after a little fussing, he got the straight-eight motor to fire up. That car, like most of Del's bikes, starts and drives.

In half the twentieth century and a decade of the twenty-first, Del has seen a lot of bikes come and go—thousands, when you count the ones he's sold as a dealer. Of all of them, none has greater meaning than that first bike he bought as a 16-year-old with his money from delivering telegrams. So strong was his memory of that bike that in 1985, he decided to build one like it to add to his collection. He bought a '47 Knucklehead and started going through it. It needed a few things, so when the chance arose to buy another one, he snapped it up. The second Harley was in pieces, which was fine for a parts machine.

Just a teenager when he bought his first ride, Del had another thing on his mind at that age: girls. As precious as his very own bike was, Del drilled holes in the front fender for a little modification that wasn't in the cycle magazines. The holes were spaced to accommodate pins on the back of some chrome letters that kids at the time used to spell out words and initials on bicycles, cars, and motorcycles. Del had picked up a pair of vowels, a pair of consonants, and that one letter that can be either one, to form "Joyce," his high school girl-

Modest though it is, as an unrestored time-capsule bike, the Aermacchi Leggero is a jaw-dropper.

friend. Such childhood memories were part of what made that bike so meaningful.

As an adult recreating that bike, Del looked through the parts that came with the second '47 Knucklehead he had just purchased. When he picked up the front fender, some isolated damage caught his eye. He ran his thumb over several oddly spaced holes and a chill ran through him—"probably the weirdest feeling I ever had in my life," Del says. He bolted into his shop and collected some chrome letters like he'd had as a kid. They matched with the holes. In his quest to reproduce the first motorcycle he owned, he had purchased that very bike, the '47 Knucklehead he bought at 16 and sold at 21. His bike was black and this one was red, so he scratched the fender. Black paint showed underneath. Then he checked the title and recognized the number. Finally, he called the bike's most recent owner and asked the name of the man he bought it from. It was the same buyer Del gave the keys to when he entered the Air Force in 1955, almost exactly 30 years before.

That bike, rough as it was and repainted, has now been restored, except for the holes in the front fender. There are no letters in them. — he didn't marry Joyce, but they will stay, a remarkable symbol of a life that was meant to be tied to motorcycles and to the Harley-Davidson Motor Company.

*"A man travels the world over in search of
what he needs and returns home to find it."*
—George Moore

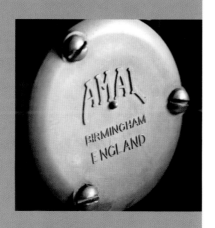

FOR A GOOD
HOME, CALL...

Speaking in superlatives is risky business because there are always undiscovered and carefully concealed examples. Let's just say this is among the lowest mileage Vincent Black Shadows.

CHAPTER 14

Mechanical Minded

Bob, Sid, and Scott Chantland's Amazing Old S#!+

THE MECHANICAL MINDED—to those who are not—are people who know how things work. If you have this disease, you know its symptoms are more serious, no easier to shake off than measles or a broken arm. To the mechanical minded, an old device with gears, levers, and shafts is not just accessible. It's irresistible. Regardless of size, purpose, or value, it will stop you, seize you, draw the full band of your intellectual powers into its quirks and cleverness. You'll study it, learn its under-lying necessity and invention, and send a mental nod across time to the craftsman who solved a problem with his hands and his wit.

When of this mind frame, you can't walk away from vintage handiwork without wishing you hadn't. Either you'll go back and study the creation or be haunted by the lost opportunity, the insight you might have gained and built upon with a little scrutiny.

The Chantlands have mechanical minds. Fascinating machines dominate their world, from the rare, the strange, the highly acclaimed, to objects as simple as a mouse trap, a pulley, or a hand-cranked butter slicer. How others value these devices is no concern to them—except that investment hunters make their lives more expensive. What matters is the genius, the passion, the skill, or sense of humor that went into producing it.

Take Sid Chantland's storage shop. With a rifle sight, you couldn't pick a line from one end to the other without a dozen car, bike, or household curiosities getting in the way. If it's old, if it's cleverly built—and especially if it's unrestored—it belongs here. As he says of his bikes, "It doesn't have to be shiny for me to love it."

In his space, a Model A with 11,000 miles sits beside a 1948 Triumph Speed Twin with 50. Behind the Ford rests an original

About the only thing not applied by the factory is the oil. Seriously. Actually, one or two little rubber John Bull cable ties have also been replaced—with NOS parts—split from age deterioration.

The 1947 125cc CZs in these crates have never been removed in more than 60 years. The photo shows a young James Dean, whose first bike was an imported CZ sold by Indian dealers to compete with Harley's 125cc model.

Excelsior whose early-style throttle and magneto linkage would delight Rube Goldberg—the straight portions of the handlebars twist, rotating flanges that move sections of straight rod through ball joints and pivoting arms from the handgrips along the bars, down the headset back along the top of the engine to the fuel and spark controls. This mechanical cable-precursor alone deserves a full minute of study. There are years of minutes here.

Five more steps and a 1916 Model T stops you cold. It wears hand-brushed black paint—now flaking, original folding top, and original seat leather, pleated, faded, and checked. A plate-glass windshield, top pane folded down, seems harmless enough, like stacked swords behind a paper screen. The only clue to its hazards is a long crack wandering across as it would on a picture window—no safety glass here, not in these original panes. Unrestored, un-"improved," this Ford is a freeze-frame of early automotive history.

In front of the untampered T is a creation no Chantland could resist: a homemade bike built from everything but motorcycle parts. The engine is 1928 Chevrolet, frame rails Model T, the radiator a modified chicken-coop heater; the fenders are their automotive counterparts reshaped and riveted, while the handlebars are cut from tubular table legs. Wheels are motorcar, the rear, only, fitted with a band brake (plan your stops a day in advance). The headset is a Model T wheel hub; steering inputs run through extended Model T steering links connecting the handlebars to the homemade fork. Spanning the nose of this beast—mottled, tapered, dented, and beautiful in its hand-fabricated homeliness—is a long tank for coolant not fuel. (The gas tank is amidship.) Nothing from *The Great Race* boasts more imagination than this bike, and it's fully functional. Sid has ridden it. He even has a photo of the farmer who created it in 1939.

Even the surrounding walls and ceiling deserve a look. Built in the early 1900s, Sid's building has served many purposes over the decades, including a casting-pattern factory. As much of the original work and craftsmanship as can be saved, will be, and Sid goes old, not new, when looking for doors, windows and details. Like his brother and father, he knows architectural salvage and antiques dealers as well as auctioneers.

Hanging out with the Chantlands is great fun because they're into everything that's cool and interesting, and they have lots of it around.

Kris Palmer

All three Chantlands own old buildings. Rough cut beams from old-growth trees, in widths and lengths unavailable today (back when a 2x4 really was 2 inches by 4 inches) have the right feel of home to this family. The lumber in their properties was hand-felled and hauled by horse teams. One plank with a sawmill's 100-year-old mark will catch a Chantland's eye—the same way they will find a pin striper's random brush marks on the bottom of a motorcycle fuel tank where he made a few strokes to remove excess paint from the bristles before striping the visible surface.

The mechanical gene comes from Bob, who began tinkering as a child. His family had no money, so at age 12 or 13, he started building his own motorbikes, affixing Briggs and Stratton engines to bicycles. The first examples had a wooden pulley that rubbed on the rear tire—no clutch development at this young age. Bob also learned the bartering art, trading up from his homemade stuff to factory-built scooters and minibikes.

Bob Chantland's Indian Chief came from a man who lived into his late 90s. The dent in the tank happened in 1948 and, like most everything else on the bike, has stayed just as it is.

Built in humble Minnesota, the Cyclone is among the most collectible motorcycles, both for the low numbers that survive and because of its remarkable overhead-cam engine. Only two whole bikes are known to exist and still bear their original paint.

His first full-size motorcycle was a '48 Indian Chief that a friend of the owner's had wrecked trying to see how fast it would go. Bob was 16 and paid $45 or $50 for the bike, which was resting on its "belly"—bent fork removed—in a large frozen puddle in a leaky shed. Bob and his father had to chisel it out and then straighten the fork, as well as possible, with a blow torch and a sledge hammer. They freed stuck valves with a liberal soaking in Liquid Wrench, whose distinctive smell to this day immediately triggers Bob's memory of working on this bike. He got it on the road, then swapped it the following year for a '57 Mercury motor to go in his '56 Ford.

In 1965, Bob purchased his first brand-new bike, a Triumph Bonneville. He rode it on the street for a year before his interest in drag

Sid Chantland calls this the farm bike, and it's among the most novel pieces in a collection marked by novelty. The South Dakota farmer who built it in the winter of 1939–40 had a great sense of purpose—and humor—as he used virtually no motorcycle parts.

racing changed the way he looked at it. Out came the wrenches and off came all parts that weren't holding it together or making it go. Bob ran at the drag strip on that bike and others for about five years, doing as well as a guy can expect with no budget and no sponsors. Mainly, it was a thrill and a chance to bond with some other guys who loved motorcycles and a mechanical challenge.

For a while, Bob had a related business making aluminum barrel castings to convert 650 Triumph engines into 750s. The go-fast crowd were interested, though not always in paying for them. "Racers wanted your stuff free," Bob remembers, "because they thought they were going to make you famous." He sold about 500 or 600 of them, a number much smaller than the potential market because he had a hard time getting quality castings. If he could have solved that problem, he figures he could have sold thousands.

Like his father, Sid got into bikes as a kid. He still has his Honda 50 MiniTrail. He spent a lot of time on dirt bikes, including trips to Mexico's Baja peninsula. In the mid-1980s, he was in the service stationed in Germany, where he capitalized on the chance to cover all of Europe by bike—a Honda XLV 750 R. Brother Scott likewise grew up with a set of handlebars never far from reach. Collecting bikes was a natural extension of riding them, and other stuff followed. Sid calls it "a hobby gone haywire" and attributes it to "bad genes," by which he means good genes. Their affliction serves motorcycle lovers past, present, and future.

This 1914 Rudge is one of the few (do we dare say the only?) known with a three-speed rear wheel hub transmission. Extremely complete unrestored condition.

Bob still has some of his racing stuff, or Sid does. Or Scott. One of Bob's old drag bikes is in Sid's building, but it might take a few seconds for them to remember who owns it. The Chantlands like the same sorts of things, and they buy and sell between themselves without necessarily moving anything. If you're fortunate enough to be exploring the collection with all three men, Bob might identify a bike, Scott will rattle off some interesting details, and Sid will announce that he recently found the receipt from when he, or Bob or Scott, bought it.

Their knowledge pool is amazing, both as to what the factories built and what they own themselves. Because they admire the same skills and ingenuity, they are equally fascinated by most everything any of them has collected. When Sid mentions that he has a DKW from World War II, Bob says that a bullet hole passes right through the exhaust pipe. Scott adds that the slug is still lodged in the engine's cooling fins. Because a bike's history is part of what makes it interesting, having three minds storing cool details keeps the collection's facts and stories well preserved, particularly for the gems.

And there are gems.

Having the Chantlands as a chapter in an unrestored motorcycle book is silly in a way. Unrestored bikes could be a section in a book on the Chantlands and all the fascinating things they own and acquire. They have dozens of motorcycles still in their original paint with the original seats, motors, wheels, and mirrors. Some have their original tires. A few have the original battery, never filled. Bob has 1940s bikes new in their original crates, unridden, unassembled, parts still wrapped in paper at factories that no longer exist by workers no longer around.

One of Bob's great finds is his 1954 Vincent Black Shadow, which a school teacher bought new in the crate in 1956. The teacher had numerous motorcycles and was a huge literature collector. He'd write to manufacturers and ask them to send him their brochures. He also amassed thousands of magazines. When he passed away, his collection went to his brother, a farmer. A friend of Bob's who used to ride Vincents when he was younger put him on to it. Bob bought 10 to 15 bikes, plus the literature, about 25 years ago. The Black Shadow has clocked only 2,597 miles and is original and unrestored, right down to the tires. To the untrained eye, it looks like a new motorcycle.

There's another prize too. Bob says, "I get great pleasure out of saying the holy grail of antique American motorcycles isn't a Harley." It's a Cyclone, made in Saint Paul, Minnesota. A dozen or so are known to exist, but most of them are Cyclone engines in an Indian or other chassis. When bikes were scrapped in the early days (the company went under in about 1916), the engine was often saved because farmers used them to run pumps and generators before electricity was widespread. Because Indian chassis are abundant and somewhat similar, they offer a means to build a Cyclone for someone with an engine. Cyclones with their original frames are scarce, and only two are known with their

The Triumph's license-plate holder has never been drilled. In a typical Triumph from this period, the plate might have a dozen holes.

A couple of days of test rides will put more miles on a brand new bike than the total mileage, 50, on this 1948 Triumph Speed Twin.

This new old stock front wheel "clip-on" motorbike engine is from the late 1940s to early 1950s. The handgrip in the foreground is the throttle.

This Triumph Thunderbird has a few more miles, and the engine's been run enough to blue the exhaust pipes. The battery has never been serviced, however. This bike, the Speed Twin, and the CZs above all originated from a Pennsylvania motorcycle dealer who tucked away oddities throughout his life.

original paint—Bob's and the bike once campaigned by Don Johns, a racer for the Cyclone factory.

Sid's sweet bikes include the Triumph above, a half dozen other rare and low mileage Triumphs, the gorgeous original-paint early Rudge pictured here, old drag bikes, scooters, and many other treats. Even modest items can be unique, like the World War II-era scooter converted to steam power by some restless innovator looking to avoid gas rationing.

These bikes merely scratch the surface of the Chantland collection, or collections, if you view them as separate entities. Bikes are just a portion of the total machinery. Sid probably has 100 mousetraps, some more than a century old, focusing mankind's creativity on a single ancient adversary. He has antique fans, too, and Scott has discovered a fondness for old refrigerators.

Together, their accumulated creations capture much of the ingenuity of the last 100-plus years. They might joke that they are captives of their sprawling possessions, but that's a modest, self-deprecating view. It's amazing what these men have amassed. If you could touch an object and travel back in time the years in its age, just imagine where this collection could take you. Touch a bike from 1910 and an 1895 mousetrap and you're back in George Washington's lifetime. Add Sid's building and Bob's and two bikes from the '40s and Christopher Columbus still lives. But there are hundreds of bikes here, plus cars, furniture, lights, signs, castings, fans, mousetraps, and sweepers. The collective age of Bob's bikes alone extends back before the time of Christ. Add Sid's, just his bikes, and you can verify the sets in *Raiders of the Lost Ark* by viewing the real pharaohs at the height of their powers.

There's so much history here, so much creativity, artistry, and genius. Just a few hours walking among these bikes makes you feel a little smarter, a little more in touch with the industrial age. Whether peculiar to you, or as familiar as your own face in the mirror, the mechanical mind is a gift to all.

Bonneville Speed Trials decals from 1968 and 1969 decorate the streamlined tank on this Triumph-powered drag bike. Burt Munro, of *The World's Fastest Indian* fame, was on hand then. The stories and the history give unrestored bikes that extra appeal. This bike is connected to the Chantlands, too, and features one of Bob Chantland's alloy 750cc conversion kits from the period.

By 1925, the motorcycle was starting to show refinement. The pedals have gone, a testament that the motor alone can handle the job. The girder fork looks similar to a springer but has no pivot point down by the axle. Note the higher spoke count to handle the drive torque at the rear wheel.

CHAPTER 15

A Friend to the Enfield

Logan Coombs's 1925 Royal Enfield 350 and Other Brit Sweetmeats

THERE'S SOMETHING SEDUCTIVE about British bikes. The lot who developed the English language, drafted Magna Carta, invented insurance, and breed wicked good musical talent, know how to pen a motorcycle. Even when the Japanese invaded and conquered the field—a British Empire specialty—they did so with bikes heavily influenced by England's designs. British bikes cranked the throttle on the postwar world, sending many a young man to his job tallying paychecks between his drudging Triumph-, Norton-, or Beeser-free life and the road-ripping bliss beyond.

When he was 18, Logan Coombs wanted a Triumph. The one in his price range was a '68 Bonneville, fresh from the showroom floor many hard miles before. This bike had been wrecked and rebuilt by an amateur. It was a Triumph, though, within budget. Enjoying motorcycles to the fullest takes an open mind and an open eye. Logan cleaned it up, put it on a maintenance schedule, and still rides it almost every day the weather serves up something reasonable—and for an avid ice racer (not on the Bonnie), that's a pretty broad standard.

Coombs has spotted potential in many tired bikes, fixed them, and gotten years of use from them—on the road and off. He's tracked down some nice unrestored bikes, too, and brought them into the stable. A few prizes come from his favorite country of origin and builders Royal Enfield, BSA, Triumph, and Greeves.

As the 1990s settled in, Logan got the idea of buying a bike made the year he was born or earlier. In '95, he saw a 1925 Royal Enfield 350cc single in some magazine coverage of a British bike rally. A '25 met his age standard by a long shot, and this bike had won a People's

This original 350 single runs well, though the factory carburetor needs work. A replacement is fitted here.

This is the Brown and Barlow carburetor fitted in 1925. The finish looks great, yet internals need attention before it goes back on the Royal Enfield.

Choice award at the show. He hadn't attended the event, however, and there was no mention of the old 350 being for sale.

Three years later, Logan went to a Royal Enfield rally at a farm near Toronto, Canada, hosted by the bike's owner. The '25 Enfield now was available as part of a spouse-appeasement deal: The owner had another project he wanted to pick up and his wife said fine, as long as he sold something else first. Scrutinizing the bike up close, Logan thought it was a pretty neat machine. He was especially drawn to its condition. "Being unrestored was the main appeal," he says.

The finish and styling had his attention. The seller then did something, unwittingly, that made Logan more interested—concerned even. As the owner set off to ride it around the rally, he kicked at the rear stand with his heel to get it into its hanger. Because the fender relies on the locked-in stand for support during operation, it clattered around under the owner's stand-raising method. Logan only needed to hear that septuagenarian steel flailing around once to conclude, "I need to take care of that bike."

This Beeser B50 is still a competent mount off road. Scored from a Michigan bike dealer, this one looks like a full resto, but the parts and finishes are more than 35 years old.

Cosmic forces seemed to agree with him. A number of Royal Enfield loyalists had been looking at the bike throughout the day, but at the end of the rally, only Logan was still around. He cut a deal and loaded up the antique Brit, now his—more or less. Between him and full ownership lay the Canada/U.S. border, a threshold he'd thought little about until he slowed for the checkpoint at Sault Ste. Marie, Michigan.

"Customs could have stopped me," he laughs. "All I had was a piece of paper [from the seller] that said, 'I'm selling this bike to Logan.'" Sincerity must have shown in his face because the border officials were content. "They certified that that's my vehicle," Logan says.

Although he hasn't ridden it much—the clutch is "a little iffy" and the carb needs some work—the antique Enfield starts and runs. With its three-speed Sturmey-Archer gearbox, it was a good performer in its day. The cush-drive rear hub reduces driveline vibration, a design so effective, Logan notes, that even Brough Superior—the Rolls Royce of bike builders—licensed it. Not everything is advanced, however. Both the shifter and throttle are right-hand controls, so you can't dip the throttle while you shift. You pick your speed and grab your gear.

Lots of lakes, a stable of bikes, and long subzero winters. No help from Nostradamus is required to predict this sport's evolution. This is Logan's "backup" B50, which can still play hard.

The proud badge is a swan song for the B50 and BSA. Only the kick start rubber has gone rough—forgivable on a dirt toy with no electric starter.

The Enfield has both a mechanical fuel pump and a hand pump to supplement engine oiling when the motor is straining either at speed or up hills.

Unlike many bikes of its day, this '25 Brit was never equipped for night riding. Acetylene lights had been around for years before this machine was built, but for whatever reason, the original buyer opted to forego them. While those old lights look cool, Logan doesn't miss them. He thinks day-only capability led to fewer miles being put on the motorcycle.

The well-before-his-birth-year bike isn't Logan's only Royal Enfield. He was interested in the marque before that, since at least the time he came upon and bought a rough Interceptor years before. That one is not as unrestored. It had been repainted in a different color, and

Greeves embodies the eternal struggle between tradition and innovation. Builders bucked common conventions in the fork and frame, while fitting a Villiers air-cooled single that looks as if it came straight out of an Art Deco sketchbook.

Logan put it back to the correct shade using a bit of the original finish he found under the chain guard.

Through owning the Interceptor, he met the editor of the North American Royal Enfield Owner's Club magazine. Ever open to new endeavors focused on motorcycles, he told the man he would be interested in taking over the job someday. The man remembered, passed the baton when he retired, and Logan served as editor for some eight years, keeping him up-to-date on the Royal Enfield scene. It was not just coincidence but a good sign when the person who expressed the most interest in getting the '25 model away from him was his predecessor in running the magazine.

If the pre-war machine is in good shape, Logan has another unrestored Brit bike that is in superb condition. His '73 BSA B50 runs perfectly, which was his reason for buying it. He wanted to go off-road. Once he got it home, however, he had one of those moments many people lucky enough to find a time-warp bike experience. He realized it was too good—original paint, original sprockets, original chain—to tear up the woods, splash though streams, and slog through muck. This was the last year for the B50 and BSA; beating up such a great original bike felt wrong. He liked his choice, though, so he managed to find another, rougher, B50 to throw at the trails.

A blend of fresh and familiar is even stronger in a full-bike shot. There's no mistaking a Greeves for any other manufacturer's offering.

Any Anglophile interested in dirt riding knows of another British marque built for that purpose, one with an impressive championship record. Greeves brought some curious designs to the drawing board and the scrambles and trials. As their competition history demonstrates, a lot of them worked. Logan scored a 1965 example in Michigan from a dealer. Professional bike sellers—especially those with a long history—are a great place to find low and no mileage bikes when they're willing to open up the back room.

A final well-preserved Brit we pulled from the collection was his sophisticated and sporty black-and-gold Triumph Trident. This bike had a bad tank when Logan got it, but connections with dealers

present and past came through again. The former owner of Sterling Cycle Works, in Saint Paul, Minnesota, had a new old stock tank in perfect condition and just the right colors.

Logan isn't just about British bikes and classics, however. Because his favorites went out of production, he's had to look elsewhere for modern high performance. Viewing the motorcycle world as one of opportunity, he's gone down some new paths and around some different tracks from the time he first got his Bonneville. In the early years, he stuck to the streets, riding mostly on the weekends. Then he started hanging around with the owner of his favorite motorcycle shop. Every time Logan went in there, he would see race results from the magazines taped to the counter showing the shop owner's performance at his most recent event.

When Logan decided to buy the owner's old Yamaha 500, the racer told him that if Logan tried flat tracking, he'd throw in a set of race wheels free. One race was all it took for Logan to be hooked. He discovered he not only enjoyed it, he was a natural. Coming to flat-tracking with zero competitive experience, imagine his surprise when he won two championships in the over-50 class. He was as good at racing modern Japanese machines as he was at hunting down cool classic bikes from England.

One thing he realized early is that racing is not really a no-contact sport. There are times in the thick of it when he had to give a few hits, and take a few too. In racing's early days, when engine power was low,

Sitting stripped in a bone yard, this bike would still be readily identifiable as a Greeves from its aluminum I-beam front frame member. Stout leading-link fork would also stand out in a dirt bike lineup.

Along with his ice and off-road fare, Logan has some more recent British road bikes, including Triumph's Trident.

This beautiful tank was not fitted from new. It's a proper Trident piece though, bought new old stock from a former Triumph dealer. Perfect.

being small was a decided advantage. Today's bikes can move bigger men, and Logan appreciated his size when he had to fight for position. The whole controlled-slide thing came more easily than he might have expected. His years of riding—and thinking and breathing—motorcycles gave him enough balance and touch to hold the bike near its limit through the turns. It was a nice reversal, having accepted the bike shop owner's dare, for Logan to walk in a couple of years later and see his own winning results taped to the counter.

If you're always up for a new bike, or a new place to ride one, living in the Land of Lakes has an inevitable effect. Some winter the unused motorcycles in the garage, and the innumerable expanses of flat terrain free of roads and cars, are going to connect in your mind—"Hey, I can

This overhead-cam 750 triple is beautiful and functional, promising a new level of performance. The bike has run less than 5,000 total miles since new.

ride these, there." To the uninitiated, ice riding sounds like a stretch. Won't you spin out of the first turn and go skidding to a stop halfway across the lake? Not if you have the right tires. The same principle that keeps ice climbers on a glacier sticks motorcycles to a frozen lake: steel spikes. In the motorcycle's case, thousands of them. Picture a classic dirt knobby tire with several hardened picks protruding from every block of tread.

Instead of traction worse than knobbies on dirt, ice tires on their intended surface provide superlative grip. "It's like a cat running on carpet," Logan says. Pulling a wheelie in the straits is as easy on an ice racer as a superbike let loose with race tires on a perfect track day. Only caveat is, if you do go down, don't let a spinning tire strike you. Such injuries are not too common and riders know to take great metaphoric pains to avoid real ones.

There are riders and racers, wrenchers, and those who mainly collect. Coombs does it all, a fully immersed motorcycle disciple. With a bevy of British bikes from that country's golden age, he has a lot to admire, use, and tinker with—all of which he does as often as time permits. Even his profession as a sign painter carries over to pin striping and paintwork on bikes that need touching up.

If you like Britain's motorcycles, you're one of a crowd. When a good bike comes along, don't wait too long to pick up the phone. The caller who beats you just might be Logan.

The original orange paint has held up well, for the same reason, perhaps, that the decal looks thin. The prior owner enjoyed polishing the bike.

"Take My Card"

Rick Wyatt's 1960 BSA Super Rocket

"Looking for a good home" is about as original in a sales ad as "too many projects" or "baby forces sale." Can you imagine a baby, 10-gallon hat pulled low over his eyes, gesturing with a big revolver as you fill out some online form? Yet some people really are looking for a good home for a surplus motorcycle, and it's more important to them than the money they get for it. Rick Wyatt knows.

He met the original owner of his 1960 BSA Super Rocket at a motorcycle shop around 1990. The owner mentioned the bike—Rick's favorite brand—and Rick gave him his card with the oft-uttered hope: "If you ever want to sell it . . ." Whole forests have been sacrificed to business cards traded over that phrase, and seldom does a twig's worth bring in a phone call. Rick's card had twig power.

In 1995, the Super Rocket rider decided he did want to sell, and he was the type to save phone numbers. He rang Rick with the good news but got no answer. Rick had departed for an antique motorcycle meet in Farmington, Minnesota. Lots of bikes trade hands at that event, and the owner of this particular one wanted his to go to the guy he met at the motorcycle shop years ago—the one who loved BSAs. So he put the 650 Beeser in a trailer and headed to Farmington.

When the man and his bike arrived, Rick wasn't around. He was helping put on the meet and had run out for supplies. He had no idea the man was looking for him. They hadn't spoken since Rick passed off his card—one of dozens over the years. There was a good chance he would not have recognized him, but the seller picked Rick out of the crowd. He said he was ready to sell the '60 Super Rocket.

"How did you find me?" Rick asked.

173

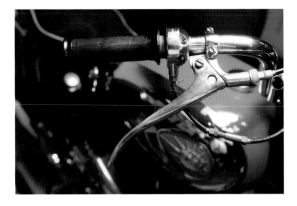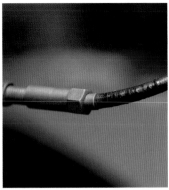

The throttle cable housing shows its age, but the cable within moves properly. Lubricating the cable reduces friction and the risk of failure.

Lots of guys go the extra mile to buy an extraordinary bike, but how many sellers pursue a buyer with the goods in tow? Although they'd discussed it, and Rick had offered to buy it, he had never actually seen the motorcycle. Even as they approached it, he couldn't view it because it was sitting in a high-sided trailer.

One mirror protruding into the air was all the casual eye could find—and a good thing too. "When I looked over the edge of that trailer, my jaw dropped. 'Oh, dear God,'" Rick mumbled. The totally stock BSA attached to the mirror was in superb condition, about the best he'd seen on a nearly 40-year-old unrestored motorcycle.

"I was immediately convinced I couldn't afford it," he says. He had just bought a '47 AJS basket case that morning. "I had maybe a hundred dollars on me. I got a real sick feeling in my stomach that I was going to lose this thing."

Sure that he couldn't come up with whatever the answer was, Rick asked, "How much?" "I know if I advertise it, I can get more," the man began. "I talked to a lot of people who know you," he continued. "If I sell it to you, you'll keep it." He then named a price that was about half what Rick thought the bike was worth.

"I was dumbfounded," Rick says, "but I had to apologize that I didn't have any money."

"Do you want the motorcycle?" the man asked. Rick said, "Of course, I want it."

It was the seller's turn to draw a card from his pocket. "Here's my number," he said. "The bike is there when you want it. Just call me." Rick offered him the hundred dollars he had left to his name as

a down-payment. The man with the Super Rocket said, "No. I know you'll come up with it."

Everything the owner said indicated that he wanted Rick and no one else to have this 650 BSA. Still, the bike was so nice and so original. It had only 17,000 miles on it. For two-and-a-half months Rick worked diligently to come up with the cash, fearful—even if there seemed no reason to fear—that someone else with a fistful of dollars might reach the seller first.

The minute he had the money, Rick called the owner. No panic. He hadn't told anyone the bike was for sale, and maybe it wasn't if Rick didn't want it. They closed the deal and the business card Rick gave the man five years before finally paid for itself, many times over.

But how many?

There are basic things a person should do when purchasing a motorcycle or any other used vehicle. It's incredible how often passion wipes those steps off the brain slate. Key in hand, cash gone away, old BSA Super Rocket now in his driveway, Rick realized he'd never kicked the starter. He saw it, loved it, bought it. He didn't even know if it worked. This from a guy with years and years of motorcycle experience.

Better late than never. He put fresh gas in it, kicked the starter, and the gleaming Beeser came to life. A shaky, sputtery life. "It ran terribly,"

A more substantial front fender hearkens to earlier styles and sits well with the larger gas tank. This is one clean bike.

Screw slots reveal that this carburetor plate has been on and off numerous times. Careful owners have left it without a significant scratch.

A little oxidation is starting to appear, which doesn't faze the owner. We all oxidize a bit after 50 years.

Rick laughs. "It shook terribly. The oil was so grungy, I decided I should pull the engine apart. This bike deserved to be as nice mechanically as it was cosmetically."

Maybe the Birmingham Small Arms gods put Rick and the original owner in the same motorcycle shop years ago for a reason. Rick has spent years rebuilding motorcycle engines, many of them BSAs. He knows them like Bond knows a Walther PPK.

"They say you never want a bike built on a Friday," he jokes. "I think this engine was built ten minutes before close on a Friday afternoon. The bike had myriad mechanical disasters. The cylinders were not bored parallel. There was a loose wrist pin. The magneto cam

ring was off so that one cylinder was way out of time with the other." He smiles. "No wonder it had only 17,000 miles."

Rick was surprised by the problems but not intimidated. Everything needed to fix the engine was right there in his shop, including the know-how. He did the required machine work, fixed the timing, and reassembled the 650 mill. Now it starts up easy and runs like it should—nice and smooth.

The original buyer had been shopping for a foster-owner to take on this bike for good. Along with the bike, he gave Rick all the important documentation, including every registration card since it was new. The early ones were cards; later, they became full-sheet titles. A few years after Rick welcomed the Super Rocket into his home, the original owner stopped by the house. He had found the original license plate. Its number matched what was typed on the original registration card. Because Minnesota allows classic vehicles to use vintage plates, the bike now runs its actual, original tag.

It isn't from 1960, however. Although the serial number confirms that this bike was built that year, it was titled as a '61. This was a convention the motorcycle shops used so that customers would feel they were getting a new bike. Rick has seen off-brands titled two or three years after their manufacturing date.

Another attribute proves this BSA is a 1960 model. The tank color, Tangerine, was available on the Super Rocket in that year alone. It came exclusively on the 4-gallon tank and was sold only to the U.S. market.

Sand and grit don't just sting bare skin. They leave their marks in the paint work too. It just proves the bike has been used and enjoyed.

The enclosed chain guard looks great. Scrapes on the drop-outs where the chain tension has been adjusted indicate that out of sight was not out of mind.

Rick Wyatt loves BSAs. This one found an ideal owner.

Most bikes that year, Rick notes, are red or blue. He has never seen another bike in Tangerine, though he has heard of guys possessing just the tank. They come available when subsequent purchasers or restorers swap to a more common color or to the smaller 3-gallon version.

Like most of us, Rick entered the motorcycle life on the cheap. His first bike, bought used—thoroughly—in 1966, was a 1948 Harley-Davidson 125. Only "bailing wire and a prayer" were keeping it together. It came with a bald rear tire on it, but the seller threw in a lugged tire in good shape.

Rick's first job was to get some tread out back. Naturally the new donut didn't fit. It went on the wheel, but it wouldn't fit under the fender. So he removed the fender. Now the tire lugs hit the frame rails. So he started trimming them off. He kept on trimming until he got the rear wheel back on the motorcycle, one of those baseline deals if you want to ride what you (regret that you) paid for. For a little margin on clearance, he hack-sawed the toolbox bracket off the frame.

Pulling off fenders always seems like an easy mod. Then you ride on wet roads and that nice wide strip of cold water and dirt up your back reminds you that fending off slop is a worthy job for a part to take on and be named for. Rick knew he was in bikes for the long haul, just not this bike.

As a child, Wyatt says, "I was always taking things apart. It was dangerous to leave tools near me." Maybe then. Today he can rebuild a motorcycle engine until it purrs better than new.

Wyatt judges bikes by the looks of their engines, and he loves the A10. The Japanese agreed with him that it was a design worthy of the highest compliment. This is the unmistakably BSA-influenced engine on Tom Jones's Kawasaki 650TT.

It's great to buy from a conscientious owner. Well after he bought the bike, Wyatt got a visit from its former keeper bearing the original plate. The title says '61, but the bike was built in 1960.

He followed the 125 with a 61-cubic inch Harley from the same year, 1948. That purchase was $200. "I way overpaid," he says. As with his first bike, this one had bad tires, so he bought a '48 Indian with decent rubber for $35. He planned to swap the tires, but the Indian ran better than the Harley. If the prices seem nominal, he was making $1 an hour then, so even the Indian cost nearly a week's wages.

"I didn't have any money," Rick remembers. "I was buying cheap junk."

He got into the British stuff in 1968 through a complicated trade involving a Triumph sports car and a Studebaker Lark. He came out of the deal with a 1956 BSA 650. It was his first motorcycle with the A10 engine, which became a favorite. "I like working on them," he says. "They're very straightforward and the separate transmission is a plus." They're easy on the eye too. "The visual aspect of the engine and transmission, the way they fall together aesthetically. . . It's a good, good-looking engine and therefore a good-looking motorcycle."

A few years later he was working with a guy who said he had a 1950 BSA 500 single. "There were a couple bikes that had made an impression on me," Rick says—"the Gold Star 500 single and Royal Enfield 500 single." A Beeser in the same displacement sounded interesting. Of course, it didn't run. It was cool, though. "I hadn't seen one like it. It had the plunger frame rear suspension. I liked it, bought it, and took it apart."

It's still apart, waiting for a slow spell to draw its owner's eyes back to that part of the shop. The mechanical work has been done since 1976. Paint's been done since 1990. "Unfortunately, I've done so many bikes for other people in between, I've never put it back together."

When it is done, it will be one of only two restored bikes Rick owns. The other is a 1950 BSA Bantam redone for his wife. Rick seldom does restorations. "My thing is the mechanical end of it. I've done mechanical work on engines in dozens of bikes—Ariel, Triumph, New Imperial, an early '30s Triumph, Indian Enfield, Brough Superior SS80."

He has about 20 motorcycles today, including a '66 Triumph TR-6, '50 Velocette 350, plus bikes from Honda, Yamaha, Kawasaki, Gilera, and BMW. He has also accumulated one of every size motorcycle BSA has built with a rigid or plunger frame suspension in the 1950s. Yet it wasn't something he planned. "I was looking around the shop one day and realized—hey, cool, how'd that happen?" he says. He has since sold the 1947 250, but to a friend. It's still around.

With all the great machines he's had through his shop, Rick's wish list is only two bikes long. The first is a pre-war BSA V-twin. "They're pretty scarce," he says. "As far as I know, they were never imported. Even in England, they're uncommon enough to be expensive. I've seen a half dozen of them over the last 35 years."

Second on the list is a 1920s BSA single with a sidecar. This one is less abstract. It's a particular bike with a particular owner, and as far as he knows it isn't for sale. But someday, he's going to drop by with a business card.

"If you have ever want to sell it . . ."

The start of it all: This 1964 Yamaha spurred a lifelong interest in riding, working on, and learning about motorcycles.

Tim O'Keeffe

CHAPTER 17

The Backroom BSA; the Passed 'Round BMW

Tim O'Keeffe's 1958 BSA C12 and 1977 R100S

No WAY. THAT WAS THE RULE at the O'Keeffe household on motorcycles and minibikes. Tim O'Keeffe's mother had lost a friend who fell off a bike and got hit by a car. The motorcycle was to blame, obviously, and none of its ilk were setting one tire on O'Keeffe land to lure its sensible folk into harm's way.

That was the rule, and Tim O'Keeffe abided it. For a while. But circumstances can affect a man, push him, change the way he thinks. Cheating death, getting girls, roaring around showing off, and road racing, trail riding, and slicing through the twisties scraping the footpegs aren't the only notions that entice a guy into the saddle. Sometimes you need to get around.

Tim was in art school in Colorado, without a car. He stayed for summer term, but his school didn't have dorms, so he was boarding at another school 8 miles away. And he was working 10 miles from there. He could take the bus to work—with enough transfers to render it just faster than walking, but his job ended at 9 p.m., as did bus service. So he hitchhiked home each night, which, depending on traffic and motorists' generosity, took from one to two hours. To make the morning's classes, he would have had to catch the 6:30 a.m. bus to school.

Even with his education incomplete, and in art, Tim could sense bad math. He was paying to learn but passing much of his days waiting at the curb, jostling in a bus seat, and wandering back roads at night trying to thumb a ride home. And he was short on sleep, chronically. He was learning all right—that he needed a car.

Surely his parents would understand the inefficiency of his current situation and also the guilt of pestering friends for rides. There had to

Although he kicked off motorcycle ownership with a 250, Tim O'Keeffe was after something much bigger when he trekked into Coney Island to look at a Triumph. The seller had already let that bike go, but he did have an attractive little Beeser.

be inexpensive options that would solve his problems and not set mom and dad back anymore than he could repay in a reasonable time. A late 1960s Mustang, or VW, for example, would get the job done nicely. All it would take was the right approach.

Or not. Do parents lose their logic as their children age, or do kids fail to grasp that the transition to adulthood requires shouldering more hardship? Tim's parents saw no need for a car loan. School was expense enough.

The risk in forcing a son to deal with his own problem is that you might not like the solution. The few hundred bucks Tim had saved from his job changing tires at Sears couldn't buy a car, at least not one that would move under its own power. He needed a more direct and dependable way around and his roommate, Art, had the answer: "You should get a motorcycle." Art's father was a hot rod builder, and while he was working on a car for his son back in high school, Art had bought a dirt bike for local transit. It was simple, cheap, durable, and got outrageous gas mileage.

But Tim wasn't interested. Maybe it was years of childhood anti-bike indoctrination. There was also a bad car-motorcycle accident Tim saw in grade school, which taught him that the biker always loses. Possibly it was just nerves. He didn't know how to ride a motorcycle. He could barely drive a stick-shift car. Only when the neurons in his brain's sneaky lobe began firing did he recognize the true value in Art's idea: blackmail.

Damp ocean air didn't harm the original paint significantly, but it did attack the signature chrome tank sides.

Convinced it was his ticket to a 1960s Mustang, Tim told his father he could only afford a motorcycle. "Good," his father replied. "What?!," Tim thought. "Put Mom on." But Dad was one step ahead. There was no violation of the no-bikes-on-O'Keeffe-land rule in Denver. Tim's father had worked for a company there and knew a motley collection of characters who all went by nicknames. One of them was into bikes. "My buddy Mugs can hook you up," his father said. Tim didn't want to be hooked up. He wanted a Mustang. Yet when the conversation was over, all he had was a piece of paper with a fresh phone number and a cartoon name on it.

There was nothing to do but go down the path he had charted. He called Mugs, who showed up in some mid-1970s land yacht, a Caddy or Continental. They took off toward the mountains, driving for miles to a new neighborhood just carved out of a hillside. Mugs and Tim pulled into a driveway and the homeowner threw open the garage door. What he rolled out changed Tim's thinking on bikes in a few sweet seconds: a gleaming blue and white 1964 Yamaha 250. It was beautiful—absolutely stunning and perfect and so much nicer than any vehicle he would have believed was in his budget. A little more small talk and Tim heard his voice say, "OK, I'll buy it."

All that remained was to pick it up, which brought back the fact that Tim had no idea how to ride a motorcycle. He asked Art to come along and handle it, but Art had to work, so Tim found another friend,

When he first saw this eager little 250 in the seller's back room, O'Keeffe was underwhelmed. His wife, Laure, loved its looks, however, and with time O'Keeffe's views have changed. She was right, of course.

Roger, who grew up with bikes. On the drive to the seller's, Tim began questioning whether the former owner would let something so nice go to a guy who couldn't operate it. Roger had the solution there, too: Tim would ride the Yamaha out of sight, after which they would trade vehicles for the rest of the trip. Roger explained the controls and feel and assured Tim that he could get the bike into first gear, putt down the road, and they'd be home free.

Back at the seller's garage, Tim paid the price and climbed aboard for his short jaunt. The launch went OK, but halfway down the road, going downhill, the layout of the controls vanished from his mind. He pulled the clutch, the engine revved, he let it go, and it lurched into a guy's front lawn, plowing into some freshly planted bushes. The man came out shouting. Tim apologized profusely as Roger hopped on the blue 250 and rode off the scene.

This O'Keeffe was now a bona fide motorcycle owner. It was the start of a long journey marked by several bikes, a few brands, and a couple of crashes, including that first Yamaha, wiped out by a drunken driver. Tim escaped shaken but not stirred, and he retained his fondness for a machine he was told he must never own.

Among those that have come since, and stayed, are two survivors true to the name: a 1958 BSA C12 250 and a 1977 BMW R100S.

The Backroom BSA

Denver was a good experience and the start of his motorcycle years, but Tim finished his education in his hometown, New York City, the nation's art, design, and publishing center. After he got his degree and had a regular income, he wanted finally to get a British bike, like a Triumph Bonnie, a quest inspired by a mechanic at his favorite Colorado parts shop, the DUMP—Denver Used Motorcycle Parts.

The mechanic had a Triumph Bitsa (bits of this and bits of that), with a funky 1950s gas tank and various Japanese parts seamlessly incorporated. Because he worked at a bike bone yard, he knew what went with what, or could be made to with a little fussing. Anything not Triumph had been artfully crafted into the machine. It made an impression on Tim as strong as the blue Yamaha.

Searching hither and yon (including trips to John's Cycle in Woodside, Queens, and calls to a Triumph dealer and repair shop, Sunrise Cycle, on Long Island) he bought a bike with "some assembly required." Hunting for the pieces to put it back together, he found an ad in a newsletter for some Triumph parts in Coney Island. It sounded worth a return to mass transit.

He and his wife, Laure, hopped the subway, then a train, then walked countless blocks to the address he'd been given. When they arrived, an older woman came to the door. She showed him in but the look was all wrong. The dominant color was a metallic gold, and the whole house was covered in plastic: plastic runways on the carpet, clear covers on the sofa and chairs. It felt more like a mafia movie set than a biker pad.

The house was the seller's mother's house, where the bike owner was camping for a while because he was getting divorced. He arrived

The original dealer sticker is frosting on a sweet bike, a reminder of O'Keeffe's New York City roots and a rare sort of badge, given the dearth of dealers in this dense urban environment.

A few nicks, pits, and chipped "teeth" mark the oil filler cap. This may be too many flaws for a restored bike, perhaps, but it's a perfect amount for one left alone.

This shop is a good 20 miles from O'Keeffe's home, but he has no reservations about riding classic bikes. That's why he owns them. During a summer festival closer to their house, he and his wife, Laure, sometimes ride the BSA down the hill and lock it to a tree. No fuss required.

shortly and took Tim to the basement door, the boundary between dust-free and grease-filled living. A few Triumphs stood out in the dimness, but they were horrible junk: butchered old bikes half fitted with chopper parts and never finished. The first one Tim scrutinized had the gas tank blurred into the frame with an ill-conceived blob of body filler.

None of these were the motorcycle and parts described in the paper. "I sold that yesterday," Basement-dweller declared. Must have figured if he got a caller out here, he might unload one of these wrecks. Tim let him know he was pretty pissed off wasting half a day traipsing out to Coney Island when the bike they discussed was no longer available.

"I got another bike in the back," his host confessed. "I was going to give it to my girlfriend."

"Girlfriend?" Tim thought. Maybe that explained the impending divorce. Of course, if she was worth the headaches and the heartache, and this motorcycle, the bike might merit a look. They went into the back room and Triumph-trasher pulled off the cover. The light glinted off a BSA 250. Tim said he didn't want that and the guy seemed taken aback. He said a friend of his in advertising wanted to rent it for a photo shoot because it's so cool. Tim asked what he'd sell it for.

"Twelve hundred bucks," the man said.

Tim felt that was an extravagant price and that the guy was looking to rip him off. He said he'd have to think about it, which meant calling John's Cycle Supply. The folks at John's sugar-coated nothing. They spoke their minds, and you could take it or leave it. Because they knew British bikes as well as anyone, more often than not, Tim listened.

Tim asked John what a BSA 250 would be worth and whether he could get parts for it. John replied, "If you paid $50, you paid $50 too much." When Tim called the seller back, he built a little bargaining room into what John said. He told the seller, "If you paid me $50 to take it, you'd be getting a good deal."

Now the seller was mad. It was a good bike, he said. "The guy I bought it from never rode it because it was too good." They went

Best buddies: BSA 250 and BMW R100S.

back and forth some more, and Tim said he'd come back out and have another look.

Laure joined him again. Despite the strange setting and the seller's self-serving tactics, she loved the little Beeser, and that can be a powerful force. Tim negotiated some more, focusing on the bike's shortcomings. The ignition switch and speedometer were missing. The seller said the speedo glass had a crack in it, so he sent it off to be fixed. More likely, thought Tim, he sold it off the bike to some other guy he had gotten out there under false pretenses.

The little BSA had come from an estate sale in Brooklyn, where the salty air had affected it. The owner's kids tried to get it running by taking off the ignition switch and bypassing it. But it was a nice bike, very original and low mileage—so he said. When the price hit a figure a fraction of the original number, Tim agreed. Laure was happy.

More parts hunting turned up a proper ignition switch and Vincent speedo that fit and looked good. Tim got the bike running and the seller had been right. It ran really nice and was, indeed, a great bike, which he'd gotten for a pretty good price when all was said and done.

In retrospect, Tim's glad he built up his mass-transit stamina in Denver. Without it, he wouldn't have bothered to huff it out to Coney Island, twice, to bargain with Goldfinger's son over the backroom BSA.

The Passed 'Round BMW

Ray and Tim met through their wives, who are both professors. The women thought their husbands would hit it off so they arranged a dinner among the four of them. Eventually the talk turned to motorcycles and the ideal bike to own.

Tim had his candidate: a Vincent Black Shadow. Ray's wife, Sarah, said a friend of hers had two or three of them, and Ray quickly added, "he's an a$$#0<€. All Vincent guys are a$$#0<€s." Strong response, from a guy Tim had just met. "OK," Tim asked, "what do you think it is?"

Ray didn't pause. "A '77 BMW R100S. It's more reliable, it's faster, and it will stop better with its disk brakes."

"How did you come up that?" Tim wondered.

"I had one," Ray said.

Several friends passed this high-performance BMW around during their college years. Apart from nominal sums and bartering, it has never really been sold—just traded hands—since the initial purchase.

The original valve covers were black, like the one on the other side of the bike. This was a replacement pulled from a Virginia floor model following a flat-tire–induced crash.

Like Tim, Ray had gone to art school, though in Virginia rather than Denver. When he started, he had to choose a medium, so Ray picked fire, a choice the school deemed "bold," "innovative," and, later, "banned," when one of his projects ignited the building. He lived on campus initially, then rented a little cabin in the Shenandoah Mountains. It had no running water, so he'd drop by his friends' house in town regularly to mooch a shower and a shave. To compensate for the sacrifices, he bought a motorcycle, a BMW R100S.

It was, according to Ray, the fastest production motorcycle in 1977. Ray rode the bike year round, shuttling himself and whatever else he needed to carry, like laundry. He also kept some of the best Kentucky moonshine made hidden in a bottle under the passenger

Most of the bike's use took place early in its life, when college years spent in the Virginia sun faded plastic and cracked rubber pieces.

It would be easy to see this licensing sticker from 1978 and conclude that the college students passing the bike around may have, er, overlooked keeping things current. We're not going to do that. Instead we'll assume there's more current documentation on the other side of the frame—somewhere.

helmet. (Cautious riders don't drink when they're out on a bike, but their medium isn't fire.)

Odd occurrences seemed to find Ray, or maybe he was good at getting in their way. One day he stopped at a bar en route to the Laundromat. When he returned, someone had stolen his dirty laundry off the BMW. Must have been someone desperate, Ray figured—curiously so, since he left the hooch. How did he know he was Ray's size, or was the thief hoping to barter for other goods with someone else's socks and underwear?

At least Ray's Bimmer was OK. He loved that bike, right up to the moment he got a flat back tire making time on a mountain highway. As any rider knows, traction departs with the air. The back end got loose and Ray tried to slow down, but things were already out of control. Through moves too quick to remember, the bike went down on its side, ground one valve cover on the asphalt, then popped back up, Ray fighting it like a bucking bronc. He got both feet down astride it and slid on his feet till his shoes were like slicks.

Bike and rider stopped at the roadside and another biker pulled up behind him. "That was so cool!" he said. No, Ray thought. It was the farthest thing from cool. He collected himself and summed up the situation. He was not really hurt, apart from some scrapes, and the bike was mostly OK. One valve cover was toast, though, and some amazing sliding and skidding hadn't fixed the back tire. Yet he was fortunate on a couple of counts more than being alive and whole.

His Bimmer had a great tool kit, and he had mopped the pavement just five miles from one of the state's two BMW dealerships. With help from the exuberant spectator, Ray got the back wheel and valve cover off and a ride to the bike shop. Although they could fix his tire, the dealer didn't have that valve cover on the shelf. Ray's luck held though, because they took one off a bike from the showroom floor. Wrong color but the right size.

Back down the road, Ray threw on the rear wheel and the new valve cover. The magic was gone, however. He fired up the bike and rode to the house where friends Tom, Scott, and Mike lived. After borrowing a little more running water to wash up, Ray set the key to the R100S on the table. It was available. Scott gave him a couple hundred bucks, and Ray walked away from his once prized possession.

He kept coming to the house as his old Bimmer made the rounds. Scott rode it awhile, then passed it to Tom. Tom put miles on it for a semester or two, and then Mike took the keys. When Ray left Virginia, it was still parked outside the house where his buddies lived.

He stayed in touch with his friends as the pass-along Bimmer faded from their topics of interest. The men were taking jobs, marrying, having kids, and getting on with adulthood's demands. Ray married Sarah, moved to Wisconsin for a time, and became friends with Tim and Laure.

One day Sarah got an email from Mike. (Ray doesn't like email.) It included the following offer:

Free to loving home
One BMW R100S motorcycle, vintage 1977
Short lineage, 29,000 original miles
Comes complete with manual and title issued to original owner
Held with loving neglect in various basements, garages, and sheds
    for the past 10 years
Must remove from property—children [becoming] old enough that
    I will not be able to deny ownership on their 16th birthdays
FOB Fort Thomas, KY

Near symmetry.
Valve covers not
withstanding.

Mike had found his two young boys out in the garage sitting on the old R100S making "vroom vroom" noises. Mike's wife is an emergency-room doctor, and her view of motorcycles is informed by the riders she's tried to reassemble. As a result, Mike wouldn't sanction his kids riding, ever, and he wanted the ability to be self-righteous when he told them so. The bike had to go, soon, while the kids were still young enough to forget they'd ever seen it.

Sarah was OK with Ray having it back, but that fire was out. She forwarded the offer to Laure with a sly "re:" line: "Don't tell Tim."

A BMW R100S, which Ray had boldly declared the most desirable bike one could own, was available—the very one Ray had bought, ridden, hidden moonshine on, had dirty laundry pilfered from, dumped in a sole-burning slide in the Shenandoah Mountains, and then passed along to all of his honorary housemates.

Over the years, Tim had gone to many places to buy bikes, or chase them. He'd been lied to as to what was available and what it cost, and he never had any sense of who had owned those motorcycles beforehand or how they'd been used. Ray's BMW was a different animal. He'd heard stories of it for years. Ray was a friend; Sarah was a friend. Tim knew the bike and its mysteries, such as why the valve covers were two different colors. He accepted Mike's offer, and he and Ray went down to Fort Thomas, Kentucky, and hauled it to Tim and Laure's home.

Now, whenever anyone asks him what the ideal bike is, Tim says, "A Vincent Black Shadow." But he can show them what his buddy Ray would say.

Index